"With a voice that is both lyrical and authoritative, this important illuminating book might be thought of as a map, or a group of maps laid out edge to edge . . . This is a book that will promote and help shape our nation's urgent conversation about race."

—JOHN ELDER, author of *Reading the Mountains of Home* and *Pilgrimage to Vallombrosa*

"Lauret Savoy's writing reveals both the pain and the hope located in landscape, place, and name. It is a wonderfully powerful and deeply personal exploration of herself, through this American landscape."

—JULIAN AGYEMAN, author of *Sustainable Communities and the Challenge of Environmental Justice*

"The personal manner and historical scenes are concise, explicit, and marvelous . . . the gentle deconstruction of the historical sources is truly moving, potent, and convincing."

—GERALD VIZENOR, winner of the Lifetime Achievement Award from the Native Writers Circle of the Americas

"How does one find a home among ruins and shards? That might be the question that leads Lauret Savoy to follow traces of life's past in landscapes, rivers, fossils and graveyards as she works to undo the silences of our nation's wounded history. As an Earth historian, she reads the land with an informed eye. As a woman of mixed heritage, she reads into the land the lives of enslaved laborers and displaced tribes. This is a work of conscience and moral conviction. Reading it I understood how the land holds the memory of our history and how necessary it is to listen to its many voices."

—ALISON HAWTHORNE DEMING, author of *Zoologies: On Animals and the Human Spirit*

"The narrator is an engaging figure, sharing with us her process of discovery, conveying her indignation without stridency (although stridency would have been justified), tracing her research, acknowledging her uncertainties, suggesting why this quest matters so deeply to herself and why it should matter to us."

—SCOTT RUSSELL SANDERS, author of
A Private History of Awe and *A Conservationist Manifesto*

"*Trace* is must-reading for anyone who cares still about life on earth right here and now. Heaven help those who follow. In her contemplative essay, Lauret Savoy locates, relocates and celebrates the majesty of America's natural landscapes . . . her loving, exhaustless examination of American language alone distinguishes this quietly powerful, nuanced, well-lit reflection. *Trace* cuts more than one gleaming, sharp-toothed key to help unlock some of the hard questions that challenge and haunt the environmental and climate-change movements."

—AL YOUNG, former Poet Laureate of California,
novelist, essayist

"Savoy . . . successfully leads readers on an illuminating journey through history—her own and her ancestors', U.S. native and nonnative peoples', and the country's, via insights on varied American landscapes and cultural and personal narratives. Savoy's immersive, accessible, and evocative narrative interweaves questions of morality, social justice, and stewardship of the land we call home with discussions of history and the American landscape and will interest readers of history, social science, and earth science."

—*Library Journal*

"First off, Lauret Savoy's sentences are beautiful. They flow with a sure diction and graceful rhythms, never a stumble or awkward turn. And they deliver plenty, whether historical or scientific information or sensory evocation. The occasional figurative image—'the residue carried downward to spread around their bases like a fallen skirt'—is always fresh and apt. She evokes rock formations and landscapes with a focus so pure and fine it seems effortless."

—JOHN DANIEL, author of *Rogue River Journal* and *The Far Corner*

TRACE

TRACE

MEMORY, HISTORY, RACE,
AND THE AMERICAN LANDSCAPE

•

LAURET EDITH SAVOY

COUNTERPOINT · BERKELEY, CALIFORNIA

LIBRARY OF CONGRESS CATALOGING-IN-PUBLICATION DATA
Savoy, Lauret E.
Trace : memory, history, race and the American landscape /
Lauret Edith Savoy.
pages 240
ISBN 978-1-61902-573-8 (hardback)
1. United States—Race relations—History. 2. United States—History—
Philosophy. 3. Memory—Social aspects—United States 4. Landscapes—Social
aspects— United States. 5. United States—Social conditions. 6. United
States--Description and travel. 7. Savoy, Lauret E—Travel—
United States. 8. Public history—United States. I. Title.
E169.Z83S38 2015
917.304--dc23
2015009588

Cover design by Debbie Berne
Interior design by Elyse Strongin, Neuwirth & Associates, Inc.

ISBN 978-1-61902-573-8

Counterpoint Press
2560 Ninth Street, Suite 318
Berkeley, CA 94710
www.counterpointpress.com

Printed in the United States of America
Distributed by Publishers Group West

10 9 8 7 6 5 4 3 2 1

CONTENTS

"Life must be lived amidst that which was made before. Every landscape is an accumulation. The past endures."

—Donald Meinig, "The Beholding Eye," from *The Interpretation of Ordinary Landscapes*

"Was that what travel meant? An exploration of the deserts of memory, rather than those around me?"

—Claude Lévi-Strauss, *Tristes Tropiques*

"Life in its creativity changes the absolute nature of time: it makes past into present—no, it melds past, present, and future into one indistinguishable, multilayered scene, a three-dimensional body. This is what ghosts are."

—Fei Xiaotong, "A World Without Ghosts"

"My life is created as I narrate, and my memory grows stronger with writing."

—Isabel Allende, *Paula*

TRACE

PROLOGUE: THOUGHTS ON A FROZEN POND

In the dead of winter I like to walk on water, held above liquid depths of the nearby lake by a vast frozen plain.

This ice demands respect. I look . . . again. Listen again . . . attentive to any *k-r-a-a-ck* or yielding to my weight. When the surface is more solid than a hardwood dance floor, and much thicker, I venture far. Even then I hear the *ga-loop*. A distant *plo-o-rp*. A muffled *gal-oosh*. Water undulating beneath ice and me.

Sunlight appears to emanate from above and below on cloudless February days, raying through the crystalline lattice underfoot. With my eyes but inches from the surface, any sense of depth, of refracted distance, yields to a sense of motion arrested. Air bubbles halt in mid-ascent. White oak leaves descend as if on invisible steps, suspended for a season above the lake bottom.

The recent past lies beneath me in these marcescent leaves, plucked and blown here by January's heavy winds. Inches away, they are out of reach. I kneel within the next stratum.

Thoughts of time's passage always come to mind on such walks, thoughts of how memory of any form becomes inscribed in the land. The hills surrounding this lake and my home are worn remains of long-vanished mountains. Glacial debris from the last ice age produces a rock-crop in my garden each spring. Stone walls that two centuries ago bordered fields and pastures now thread the dark heart of forests.

Loren Eiseley wrote in *The Immense Journey* that human beings are denied the dimension of time, so rooted are we in our particular now. We cannot in person step backward or forward from our circumscribed pinpoints. I cannot touch a leaf encased in ice—nor can I feel the calloused hands that stacked these walls. Yet we make our lives among relics and ruins of former times, former worlds. Each of us is, too, a landscape inscribed by memory and loss.

I've long felt estranged from time and place, uncertain of where home lies. My skin, my eyes, my hair recall the blood of three continents as paths of ancestors—free and enslaved Africans, colonists from Europe, and peoples indigenous to this land—converge in me. But I've known little of them or their paths to my present. Though I've tracked long-bygone moments on this continent from rocks and fossils—those remnants of deep time—the traces of a more intimate, lineal past have seemed hidden or lost.

Yet to live in this country is to be marked by its still unfolding history. *Life marks* seen and unseen. From my circumscribed pinpoint, I must try to trace what has marked me. The way traverses many forms of memory and silence, of a people as well as a single person. And because our lives *take place* among the shadows of unnumbered years, the journey crosses America and time.

Come with me. We may find that home lies in *re-membering*—in piecing together the fragments left—and in reconciling what it means to inhabit terrains of memory, and to be one.

Lauret Edith Savoy
Leverett, Massachusetts

Trace.

NOUN. A way or path.

A course of action.
Footprint or track.
Vestige of a former presence.
An impression.
Minute amount.
A life mark.

VERB. To make one's way.

To pace or step.
To travel through.
To discern.
To mark or draw.
To follow tracks or footprints.
To pursue, to discover.

THE VIEW FROM POINT SUBLIME

One journey seeded all that followed.

We had entered Grand Canyon National Park before sunrise, turning west onto the primitive road toward Point Sublime. This was in those ancient days when a Coupe de Ville could negotiate the unpaved miles with just a few dents and scrapes. My father had driven through the Kaibab Plateau's forest on Arizona Highway 67 from Jacob Lake, Momma up front with him. No other headlights cut the dark. I sat in the backseat with Cissie, my dozing eighteen-year-old cousin. Our Kodak Instamatic ready in my hands, cocked. For two hours or more we passed through shadows that in dawn's cool arrival became aspen-edged meadows and stands of ponderosa pine. Up resistant limestone knolls, down around sinks and ravines. Up then down. Up then down. In time, through small breaks between trees, we could glimpse a distant level horizon sharpen in the glow of first light.

Decades have passed, nearly my entire life, since a seven-year-old stood with her family at a remote point on the North Rim. I hadn't known what to expect at road's end. The memory of what we found shapes me still.

POINT SUBLIME TIPS a long promontory that juts southward into the widest part of the canyon, a finger pointing from the forested

Kaibab knuckle. It was named by Clarence Edward Dutton with other members of field parties he led between 1875 and 1880, first on John Wesley Powell's Geographical and Geological Survey of the Rocky Mountain Region, then under the new U.S. Geological Survey. To Dutton the view from the point was "the most sublime and awe-inspiring spectacle in the world."

The year the Grand Canyon became a national park, in 1919, more than forty-four thousand people visited. Most of them arrived by train to the South Rim. On the higher and more remote North Rim, those daring could try wagon tracks used by ranchers and "pioneer tourism entrepreneurs" over rough limestone terrain to Cape Royal and Point Sublime. Or they could follow a forest service route to Bright Angel Point. Soon roads scratched out on the Kaibab Plateau would replace the old wagon paths, allowing work crews to fight fires as well as infesting insects.

But the summer of 1925 would be a turning point. For the first time, and ever since, visiting motorists outnumbered rail passengers. The National Park Service encouraged and responded to this new form of tourism by building scenic drives and campgrounds on both rims. Auto-tourists often attempted the twisting, crude road to Point Sublime.

The Grand Canyon now draws nearly five million visitors each year. The seventeen-mile route to Point Sublime remains primitive, and sane drivers tend not to risk low-clearance, two-wheel-drive vehicles on it. Sometimes the road is impassable. One year it was reported to have "swallowed" a road grader. Still, the slow, bumpy way draws those who wish to see the canyon far from crowds and pavement, as my father wanted us to do those many years ago.

None of us had visited the canyon before that morning. We weren't prepared. Neither were the men from Spain who, more than four hundred years earlier, ventured to the South Rim as part of an *entrada* in search of rumored gold. In 1540 García López de

Cárdenas commanded a party of Coronado's soldiers who sought a great and possibly navigable river they were told lay west and north of Hopi villages. Led by Native guides, these first Europeans to march up to the gorge's edge and stare into its depths couldn't imagine or measure its scale. Pedro de Castañeda de Nájera chronicled the expedition:

> They spent three days on this bank looking for a passage down to the river, which looked from above as if the water was six feet across, although the Indians said it was half a league wide. It was impossible to descend, for after these three days Captain Melgosa and one Juan Galeras and another companion, who were the three lightest and most agile men, made an attempt to go down at the least difficult place. . . . They returned about four o'clock in the afternoon, not having succeeded in reaching the bottom on account of the great difficulties which they found, because what seemed to be easy from above was not so, but instead very hard and difficult. They said that they had been down about a third of the way and that the river seemed very large from the place which they reached, and that from what they saw they thought the Indians had given the width correctly. Those who stayed above had estimated that some huge rocks on the sides of cliffs seemed to be about as tall as a man, but those who went down swore that when they reached these rocks they were bigger than the great tower of Seville.

The Spaniards knew lands of different proportions.

Writing more than three centuries later, Clarence Dutton understood how easily one could be tricked by first views from the rim. "As we contemplate these objects we find it quite impossible to realize their magnitude," he wrote. "Not only are we deceived, but we are conscious that we are deceived, and yet we cannot conquer the deception." "Dimensions," he added, "mean nothing to the senses, and all that we are conscious of in this respect is a troubled sense of immensity."

Point Sublime holds a prominent place in Dutton's *Tertiary History of the Grand Cañon District*, the first monograph published by a fledgling U.S. Geological Survey in 1882. Lavishly illustrated with topographic line drawings and panoramas by William Henry Holmes, Thomas Moran's paintings and drawings, and heliotypes of Jack Hillers's photographs, it is an evocative work from a time when specialized science hadn't yet constrained language or image. The monograph also shows a science coming of age. For in the plateau and canyon country, aridity conspired with erosion to expose Earth's anatomy. The land's composition and structure lay bare. Though terrain was rugged and vast, equipment crude or lacking, these reconnaissances tried to sketch plausible models for land-shaping forces. Clarence Dutton gazed out from the North Rim at Point Sublime to describe the grand geologic *ensemble*: the great exposed slice of deep time in canyon walls, the work of uplift and erosion in creating the canyon itself. Dutton also brought his readers to the abyss's edge to see with new eyes.

The men on the surveys by and large beheld with eastern eyes, responding at first with senses accustomed to the vegetative clothing of a more subdued, humid land. They saw at a time when various meanings of "the sublime" had become essential to how the educated in Europe and their descendants in America conceived of the world about them. In a Romantic sublime one encountered power greater than imagined or imaginable. One beheld the might and presence of the Divine. On a mountain peak. In a great churning storm. At the brink of a fathomless chasm. To come to the edge of the Grand Canyon and experience the sublime was to feel unsettled, deeply disoriented. To be awestruck. "In all the vast space beneath and around us there is very little upon which the mind can linger restfully," Dutton wrote. "It is completely filled with objects of gigantic size and amazing form, and as the mind wanders over them it is hopelessly bewildered and lost."

But he didn't stop there. Dutton realized that objects disclosing "their full power, meaning, and beauty as soon as they are presented to the mind have very little of those qualities to disclose." After many field seasons he came to see the "Grand Cañon of the Colorado" as "a great innovation in modern ideas of scenery, and in our conceptions of the grandeur, beauty, and power of nature." Such an innovation couldn't be comprehended immediately. "It must be dwelt upon and studied, and the study must comprise the slow acquisition of the meaning and spirit" of the country.

> The lover of nature, whose perceptions have been trained in the Alps, in Italy, Germany, or New England, in the Appalachians or Cordilleras, in Scotland or Colorado, would enter this strange region with a shock, and dwell there for a time with a sense of oppression, and perhaps with horror. . . . The tones and shades, modest and tender, subdued yet rich, in which his fancy had always taken special delight, would be the ones which are conspicuously absent. But time would bring a gradual change. . . . Great innovations, whether in art or literature, in science or in nature, seldom take the world by storm. They must be understood before they can be estimated, and they must be cultivated before they can be understood.

The author Wallace Stegner wrote his dissertation on Clarence Dutton, later referring to him as "almost as much the *genius loci* of the Grand Canyon as Muir is of Yosemite." Tourists visiting the park might not be aware of the debt owed, but Stegner believed "it is with Dutton's eyes, as often as not, that they see." While residents of eastern landscapes might have spurned canyons and deserts as irredeemably barren, Dutton's words and vision helped change the terms of perception. That is, for an audience acquainted with particular notions of the sublime and nature, an audience with the means, time, and inclination to tour.

. . .

What did my family bring to the edge and how did we see on that long-ago morning? I've wondered if the sublime can lie in both the dizzying encounter with such immensity and the reflective meaning drawn from it. Immanuel Kant's sublime resided in the "power in us" that such an experience prompted to recognize a separateness from nature, a distance. To regard in the human mind an innate superiority over a natural world whose "might" could threaten flesh and bones but had no "dominion" over the humanity in the person. In Kant's view, neither I nor my dark ancestors could ever reach the sublime, so debased were our origins. In Kant's view neither could W. E. B. Du Bois, for whom this "sudden void in the bosom of the earth," which he visited half a century before us, would "live eternal in [his] soul."

We had little forewarning of where the Kaibab Plateau ended and limestone cliffs fell oh so far away to inconceivable depth and distance. The suddenness stunned. No single camera frame could contain the expanse or play of light. Canyon walls that moments earlier descended into undefined darkness then glowed in great blocky detail. As shadows receded a thin sliver in the far inner gorge caught the rising sun, glinting—the Colorado River.

I'll never know what that morning meant to my father when he took this detour on his homeward journey. Or to my mother. We traveled together but arrived with different beholding eyes.

This was The Move. My parents were returning to a familiar and familial East. My home lay behind us on the sunset coast, where I was born at the elastic limit of my father's last attempt to craft a life far from Washington, D.C. Movement and change had occurred often—from San Francisco to Los Angeles, from rented bungalow to apartment to second-story flat. The last to 1253 Redondo Boulevard. But these were small steps, our lives pacing an unchanged rhythm. Momma worked as a surgical nurse, mostly night shifts. Dad did many things—marketing, public relations, jobs I never really knew. We lived by what I now know were modest means, each home furnished with what was necessary, accented by his ceramics, pastels, paintings, handmade table and lamp.

In a neighborhood with few children, my reliable companions were sky's brilliant depth and the tactile land. The Santa Monica and San Gabriel Mountains shaped the constant skyline north and west.

If a child's character and perceptual habits form by the age of five or six, then I perceived by sharp light and shadows. If a child bonds with places explored at this tender age, and those bonds anchor her, then I chose textures and tones of dryness over humidity, expanses that embraced distance over both skyscraper and temperate forests.

So when my father, nearing fifty years of age, decided to return to Washington, D.C. to try again, I told my parents to leave me behind. We had visited his family there; I wanted no more of it.

But a seven-year-old has little choice short of running away. If I could gather sunlight and stones, if I could keep Pacific Ocean water from spilling or drying up, then home could come with me.

Sifting through memory's remains—of words spoken, decisions made, actions taken—feels like the work of imagination in hindsight. The scaffolding that ordered my world stood on happenstance. That because my father decided we'd drive across country in a leased Cadillac, roomy and comfortable enough for four; because he chose to stop at national parks on the way—because of these things I stood at that edge, a small child with a Kodak Instamatic in hand.

Those moments at Point Sublime illuminated a journey of and to perception, another way of measuring a world I was part of yet leaving behind. I felt no "troubled sense of immensity" but wonder—at the dance of light on rock, at ravens and white-throated swifts untethered from Earth, at a serenity unbroken.

The ocean I'd tried to bring across country had evaporated. Sunlight wouldn't be contained. But pebbles came willingly. Limestone joined basalt, sandstone, and granite on the rear window mat. Images of the canyon, Kaibab Plateau forest, and Colorado River thickened the growing stack of postcards.

EROSIVE FORCES CARVED the North Rim's edge. My family crossed many edges that summer. West to East. One childhood home left for another. Before to after. History began for me on The Move. What preceded was a sense of infinite promise and possibility in a world that made sense. What followed promised nothing. Daddy hoped the nearing future would be a return to origins and dignity. My soon constant question to him, "When are we going home?" always met the same response: "We are home."

My bearings lay in memories of bright days, in snapshots and postcards, stones and a salt-encrusted jar. By the age of ten I knew it was better not to want anything too badly.

I've tried to return to Point Sublime many times. Fire danger and an impassable road aborted all but two attempts. The wooden post still stands, but without the carved sign that marked our presence in a photograph from that distant morning. POINT SUBLIME ELE-VATION 7464. Three of us face morning light; our shadows stretch toward the edge, oblique dark columns. Dad leans against the sign, his mouth caught in midsentence. Cissie stands next to him, her Uncle Chip. In front of them, in pressed pants and first-grade uniform blouse and sweater, a child looks down and away. She waits for the shutter to click.

Good morning, yesterday. Gazing into this image, I see us as my mother did—then beyond, toward the abyss. I know our future.

Now my father's age then, I am a witness from a later time checking the rearview mirror. Most of my life has taken place in the East for reasons that at moments of decision seemed right. It's impossible to step into that bright summer morning again, attentive to it, to parents alive, to an intact family drawn by hope and promise. Point Sublime remains. I still try to negotiate its terrain.

PROVENANCE NOTES

Seven years old on a sun-bright June day, she stands by the curio shop's postcard rack. In their move across country her parents have visited many national parks—Sequoia, Kings Canyon, Zion, the Grand Canyon's North Rim—and at every stop made, for gassing up or seeing sights, she runs first to the postcard rack. Turning through metallic squeaks she seeks more images of home, a vision grown beyond California's coast to canyons, deserts, and mountains of her West. These places must come east, too.

Ten cents a card. She takes selected treasures to the cashier: Point Imperial at sunrise; goldening aspen groves; layered, dusklit canyon walls; brick-red river against brick-red rock. Light, texture, home.

The woman behind the counter tilts her head but greets a man approaching the register. She will help him. Marlboros. Then another customer. Postcards and questions about road conditions and nearby motor courts.

The girl stands quietly, her head at counter level. These people act as if she isn't there. Through the display glass she examines polished stones and beaded place mats under sunlit dust. The room smells stale.

Only after all others have gone does the woman behind the counter extend her hand. Six cards, sixty cents. When the girl reaches up with three quarters the woman avoids the small hand to take the coins. Cash register clinks shut. The woman turns away.

The girl starts to ask but stops as the woman faces her. At seven she doesn't yet know contempt or refusal, and runs far into the pine-woods behind the store. That night, with all her home-cards covering the motel bed, she wonders if each bright place is enough.

SAND AND STONE are Earth's memory. Old worn postcards keep a child's memory safe in my desk. Stanley Kunitz wrote in his poem "The Testing-Tree" that "the heart breaks and breaks and lives by breaking." At a young age I began to hope that despite wounds a sense of wholeness could endure. That each of us possesses a *hardness*—not harshness, not severity, but the quality of stone or sand to retain some core though broken again and again.

This child-hope remained hollow of adult understanding until my second journey across country alone some years ago. After two months on the road I reached Southern California, the point of return. A threshold to memory opened in crossing the Mojave Desert to the Devil's Punchbowl.

Steeply tilted sandstone ledges hundreds of feet high rim the Punchbowl, a "geologic curiosity" within the San Andreas Fault zone. Fluent and patient in its work, the small stream draining the rocky bowl gathers and reworks pieces of the cliffs and abutting San Gabriel Mountains, today as it has done through centuries of days. It is a tactile reminder that here is a land of process and response. From cloud to creek, the motive forces of water—the forces of weathering and erosion—and abrasive, shuddering movements along bounding faults shaped and continue to reshape the cliffs and basin. What one might perceive as timeless is but one frame of an endless geologic film.

I descended through stands of pinyon, manzanita, and mountain mahogany to wade the cooling water. To watch grain after entrained sand grain roll, bounce, and be carried aloft. Long-avoided questions emerged as the current nudged me downstream with its sediment. I was five years old when last at the Devil's Punchbowl, on a picnic with my mother and father. Decades later the cliffs and basin still fit within memory's frame, satisfying a wish to feel sun-warmed sandstone and this stream's grainy flow. But perhaps I also returned to reach beyond memory to some origin, to some direction. That five-year-old had imagined these waters flowed from the beginning of the world.

Odysseus said, "I belong in the place of my departure and I belong in the place that is my destination." I hadn't known either place, fear stilling me for years. But the Punchbowl's ledges, this stream, and the shaping faults seemed to *re-turn* me to an awareness I couldn't reach alone. That long-ago picnic fired a child's passion to inhabit stories the land held—stories that assumed great importance as I grew up in a family with little spoken memory.

. . .

The San Gabriel Mountains rise to ten thousand feet, jutting high above Los Angeles and the Mojave Desert. Between peaks and city basin lies the sharp turning hinge of a geologic trap door hidden by alluvium, freeways, and sprawl. These mountains continue to lift at rates among the fastest on the continent. But as they grow, they weather away, grain by grain, the residue carried downward to spread around their base like a fallen skirt. The daily business here is uplift and erosion, mountain-making and decay.

The nearby Devil's Punchbowl consists of sandstone and conglomerate, once sands and pebbles of ancient mountain streams that flowed millions of years ago, now upended into rocky tablets.

What to take from this?

Each grain, each pebble embedded in Punchbowl rock, began as detritus from the denuding of ancestral highlands. Now-vanished cascades once conveyed sand and gravel down now-vanished mountains. If you and I were to examine the pieces, consider their texture and makeup, we could deduce much about their places of origin, about climate through time. But the Punchbowl as a place of tilted rock also means later shifting and deforming. Earthquake after earthquake dragged and shoved this terrain against the San Gabriel Mountains like a crumpled carpet shoved into a wall.

Origin and material source. Warping displacement. We can still detect both kinds of provenance even though most of what once existed long since eroded away.

What of us? What of who we are is owed to memories of blood or culture, custom or circumstance? To hardness? What makes an individual in a sequence of generations?

These questions simmered on my drive east from the Punchbowl. June edged toward its longest days as I followed Pacific-bound streams to their source, then across the Continental Divide. It did seem easier to piece together the geologic history of almost any place on Earth than to recover my ancestors' past. Easier to construct a plausible narrative of a long-gone mountain range from the remnant pieces than to recognize the braiding of generations into a family. Than to know my parents' reasons for turns taken.

FROM WHAT DO we take our origin? From blood?

I am the child of a woman with deep brown skin and dark eyes who married a fair-skinned man with blue-gray eyes. Yet as a little girl in California I never knew race. Skin and eye color, hair color and texture, body height and shape varied greatly among relatives. Like the land, we appeared in many forms. That some differences held significance was beyond me. Instead I devised a self-theory that golden light and deep blue sky made me. Sun filled my body as it seemed to fill dry California hills, and sky flowed in my veins. *Colored* could only mean these things.

On that drive east from the Punchbowl I realized how little I knew of my family as an organic unit held together by shared blood, experience, or story. I was born to parents already in middle age. They had come into the world before moving pictures talked, before teamsters drove only horseless trucks, before the iceman had to find a new profession. And they'd lived with elders who could recall life before the Civil War, memories lit by lantern light. Though nearly palpable, their pasts never spoke to me. Dad died before I had the questions. In response to them, Momma said she couldn't remember. She wondered why I wanted to know.

FROM WHAT DO we take our origin? From incised memories?

Near the end of her life my father's mother visits us in California, sharing my room. I'm nearly five years old. Slow, tidy with words and her things, ancient to me, Gu-ma brushes her graying chestnut hair each day. It falls below her knees. I like to lean into the back of her thighs, grasping her legs to feel her flesh warm my face. Gu-ma's hair covers me, hides me. Each night I pray for long straight hair like hers, and for her eyes—my father's eyes—so I might see through sky, too.

Second-grade recess, Campus School playground, Washington, D.C. I stand by empty swings. A classmate walks up to say "You're colored, aren't you?" I nod yes to what really isn't a question. Troubled by how ugly Bobby Kane could make sun-light and sky-blue sound, I run to Sister Mary Richard Ann. That evening I ask my parents.

Home, many a workweek night. My father sits in his easy chair, alone in the back room, a glass of gin or scotch in one hand, cigar or cigarette in the other. The only light the inhaling burn. What he sees or thinks, I don't know. What I remember? Smoke. Silence.

Lessons in fifth-grade social studies, Dunblane Catholic School.

One: Our textbook describes the unsuitability of Indians, who wasted away, and the preference for Africans, who thrived as slaves and by nature want to serve. I ask my teacher, Mrs. Devlin, if I might become a slave.

Two: We read in class that Indians are savages who had to give up the land and their wasteful way of life for the sake of civilization. The book calls this part of Manifest Destiny. Confused again, I ask what made the "five civilized nations" civilized?

Imagine searching for self-meaning in such lessons. Am I civilized? Will I be a slave? The history taught wasn't the history that made me, but I didn't know this. Any language to voice who I was, any knowledge of how land and time touched my family, remained elusive.

Once we moved to Washington, D.C., in the late 1960s, I came to learn how "race" cut our lives. *Black, Negro, nigger!* came loud and hard after the 1968 riots. Words full of spit showed that I could be hated for being "colored." By the age of eight I wondered if I should hate in return.

WHAT I COULDN'T grasp then was that twining roots from different continents could never be crammed into a single box. I descend from Africans who came in chains and Africans who may never have known bondage. From European colonists who tried to make a new start in a world new to them. As well as from Native peoples who were displaced by those colonists from homelands that had defined their essential being.

As the nineteenth century ended, family members by blood and marriage had dwelled in rural Virginia, Maryland, Alabama, perhaps Oklahoma, and Montana ranchland along the Yellowstone River. They came to live in cities like Washington, D.C., and Harrisburg, Pennsylvania. But how they experienced the world or defined themselves in it remained unknown. Forced removal, slavery, and Jim Crow were at odds with propertied privilege. Forebears had likely navigated a tangled mélange of land relations: inclusion and exclusion, ownership and tenancy, investment and dispossession. Some ancestors knew land intimately as home, others worked it as enslaved laborers for its yield. What senses of belonging were possible when one couldn't guarantee a life in place? Or when "freed" in a land where racialized thinking bounded such freedom?

As I crossed the Continental Divide, the questions became so urgent they soon composed the journey. High in Colorado's Rocky Mountains, where the Arkansas River rises, I decided to try to trace family, and myself, from storied places and recorded history. But *where* to start?

Watching the Arkansas's headwaters begin to carry mountain detritus toward the plains, I suspected *this* river could guide me. So by its drainage I plotted a meandering course toward Oklahoma, where an elderly cousin of my mother's had once told me some ancestors might have lived.

SAND CREEK. THE name-shadow long pulled, its memory contested since November 29, 1864. As that dawn broke, several hundred volunteer soldiers led by John Chivington attacked a large Cheyenne and Arapaho encampment along its waters. Black Kettle and other leaders had thought they were under U.S. Army protection by land reserved for them. Most of the troops and Colorado territory settlers would memorialize what happened as a glorious battle against hostile foes. To survivors it was a massacre of about two hundred companions, most of them women, children, and elderly. On Chivington's alleged orders—"Kill and scalp all, big and little; nits make lice"—attackers mutilated corpses, taking scalps and other body parts as trophies. Heads shipped to the Army Medical Museum later ended up in the Smithsonian Institution's collections.

It was by a sense of "how could I not" that I entered eastern Colorado's plains in search of this winding tributary of the Arkansas River.

State Highway 96 and the Missouri Pacific Railroad tracks cross Big Sandy Creek just east of the ruined town of Chivington. No cars, no person passed in the hours I walked along the bank, through high grass and over barbed wire, as the stream bent through shallows and riffles across the plains. Killdeer and red-winged blackbirds were my only vocal companions besides cottonwood leaves shuddering in a constant June-dry wind. A century and a half before, a breeze lifted a U.S. flag by Black Kettle's lodge. Villagers waved white flags at the approaching troops.

That no roadside marker acknowledged the violence didn't surprise me. The land hadn't yet opened to the public as a historic site under the National Park Service. Nothing appeared on my road map or atlas-gazetteer. The slaughter wasn't mentioned in my schoolbooks. Neither was the muddied water sweeping earth to the horizon, nor the shadows I tried to follow.

WHILE THUMBING AN issue of *Colorado Heritage* magazine at a rest stop, I chanced across possible treasure. One O. E. Aultman had opened a photographic studio in Trinidad, Colorado, in 1889. Among nearly five thousand surviving images were stunning portraits of African Americans and people of obviously mixed heritage.

Surely Trinidad, founded where the Santa Fe Trail's northern route
and Purgatoire River converged, was also a place where many peoples had converged. I had no idea if any of my ancestors had passed
this way, but I'd learn what I could.

Both the director of the Trinidad History Museum and a volunteer at the A. R. Mitchell Museum of Western Art were gracious and
apologetic.

*Little information is left on African Americans in this area—of
course, they don't live here now . . .*

*Subject information for the Aultman photos is almost non-existent,
the titles of many images are just* Unidentified____.

Unidentified, unidentifiable. Like isolated grains of sand, these
photographs teased absent stories. The town had just begun its
big festival to celebrate the opening of the Santa Fe Trail. People
crowded the streets. No one looked like me.

. . . of course, they don't live here now.

I left Trinidad, returning east, downstream to the Arkansas.

MANY RIVERS BECOME one in Oklahoma. The Cimarron, forks
of the Canadian, and Salt Fork vein eastward across the state to
join the Arkansas before it meanders between Ouachita and Ozark
uplands. I drove in with an evening thunderstorm, crossing the
hundredth meridian between the Cimarron River and Canadian
North Fork. Rolling plains greened almost secretly.

I couldn't remember being in Oklahoma before; maybe familial
memory remained. My mother's cousin had told me years before
that kin might have come here, that they were Black Cherokee or
Creek. Whether she was right or wrong, I knew only some surnames: Turner, Reeves, Cade, and Allen.

A road sign declared YOU ARE ENTERING I.T.

Enslaved African Americans once lived in "Indian Territory." They'd been brought by members of the Cherokee, Chickasaw, Choctaw, Creek, and Seminole nations forced across the Mississippi River in the southeastern removals of the 1830s and 1840s. Although only an elite few of the "five civilized tribes" held human beings as property, more than seven thousand people with African blood lived in bondage in Indian Territory on the eve of the Civil War. But bondage took different forms, from the rigid "slave codes" of the Cherokee Nation to more fluid social relations in Seminole society.

Autonomous communities of Seminole "slaves" formed the earliest Black towns here. Freed people established more settlements after the war. Then came the 1889 and 1890s land runs. Thousands of African American homesteaders were among those who settled "unassigned" or "surplus" lands—what hadn't been reserved for other removed tribal peoples including Cheyenne, Arapaho, Comanche, and Apache. Many settlers came from the Deep South searching for what one Black territorial newspaper called "the last chance for a free home." By 1910 at least thirty all-Black towns had formed in what was now the new state of Oklahoma, most striving to become independent, farm-supported communities. Those now abandoned—like North Fork Colored, Cimarron City, Liberty, or Wybark—rival in number those surviving—like Summit, Tullahassee, Boley, and Langston City.

I had no idea where my mother's family fit in, if at all.

ROLLING AND GULLIED red plains lie south of the Cimarron River in north-central Oklahoma. Langston City began there in 1890 on unassigned lands opened in the 1889 run. Its population once exceeded three thousand—before the state highway was rerouted.

I spent a day gathering what information I could in the Black Heritage Center archives of Langston University, formerly the

Colored Agricultural and Normal University of Oklahoma. Through the 1890s and early 1900s, Langston City's founder, Edwin P. McCabe, and other leaders promoted a "Negro" Oklahoma. They advertised existing towns and recruited immigrants for new town colonies and homesteads. "Langston City restores to the Negro his right and privileges as an American citizen and offers protection to themselves, families, and home," wrote McCabe, also editor of *The Langston City Herald*. "Langston City is the Negro's refuge from lynching, burning at the stake and other lawlessness and turns the Negro's sorrow into happiness."

The hope that Oklahoma might be admitted to the Union as an African American–controlled state was far from fancy for thousands of Black homesteaders. But the promise of self-governing havens would be dashed. Owners of small farms had little margin against drought or repeated crop failures. Few could afford the turn to mechanized farming. And when Indian and Oklahoma territories became the state of Oklahoma in 1907, the legislature disenfranchised African American residents and segregated public facilities.

OKFUSKEE COUNTY. ALTHOUGH it appeared that I-40 had sucked the life from Highway 62 in rural east-central Oklahoma, the road sign was enough to draw me in:

WELCOME TO BOLEY
LARGEST AFRICAN AMERICAN TOWN
FOUNDED 1903
BOLEY RODEO MEMORIAL WEEKEND

The historical marker clinched it: BOLEY, CREEK NATION, I.T., ESTABLISHED AS AN ALL BLACK TOWN ON LAND OF CREEK INDIAN FREEDWOMAN ABIGAIL BARNETT . . .

The wide main street was empty of cars, the stone-and-brick buildings lining it more boarded up than not. I almost didn't stop. But at Boley's Community Center I met Mrs. M. Joan Matthews, mayor, and her sister Mrs. Henrietta Hicks. They gave me a tour of the town "museum," an old house opened on request.

From these generous women and other residents, I learned that Boley began as a rural community of Creek freed people following the Civil War. Formally established as a town after the turn of the twentieth century, it quickly became "a going concern," with more than four thousand residents.

Like *The Langston City Herald*, *The Boley Progress* found its way throughout the South, promoting the town as a refuge. "Have you experienced freedom?" began one early article. "What are you waiting for? If we do not look out for our own welfare, who is going to do it for us? Are you always going to depend upon the white race to control your affairs for you?" ran another.

By 1912 Boley boasted two banks, five grocery stores, five hotels, seven restaurants, three or four cotton gins, three drugstores, one jewelry store, four department stores, two livery stables, two insurance agencies, two photographic studios, two colleges, plus a lumberyard, ice plant, electrical generating plant, funeral home, newspaper, post office, and railroad depot. Its Masonic temple was the tallest building around for some time. Visiting a few years earlier, Booker T. Washington had praised Boley as the "most enterprising, and in many ways the most interesting of the Negro towns in the United States."

Now the population hovers around a thousand. The main employers, I was told, are a nearby prison and the Smokaroma, on Bar-Bq Avenue. The town's biggest event, the "oldest existing rodeo in an African American community."

Everyone I met in Boley was warm and welcoming. Still I felt an unbridgeable distance. These people *know*. They were born here;

they've lived here all their lives. They know their past. They know home. The names of the Creek freed people who founded the town didn't include names I knew.

A century and more ago it was *Come to Boley! Come to Cimarron City! Come to Liberty!* Did ancestors come? I imagined some of my mother's forebears relocating from Alabama's water-thick air, plantation fields, and dark woods. I imagined their response to expanses of grass and sky, to the opening of distance to the eye, to a land on which they hoped to live on their own terms. I imagined the difference in felt attachment to place that one generation could make—one born in the antebellum South, another on the plains.

Had they wagoned in on a day like that of my visit, the sky an open vault, the air scented by the previous night's rain and a thick June greening, they *must* have imagined possibility and then begun to live it. I'd like to say the old homestead lay upstream, that they called it *haven*, that maybe they raised broodmares and grew the best greens for miles. I'd like to believe imagination could be sparked by familial memory.

Or did any arrive in bondage decades earlier as slavery and enslaved were brought westward on trails of tears? Were any of them "Buffalo Soldiers" posted at Fort Sill or Fort Reno? Companies from the army's then all-Black regiments served a century and more ago in Indian Territory.

I imagined but did not know.

Boley elders suggested looking for family names in the Dawes allotment rolls of the five nations. So east I drove to Okmulgee, capital of the Muskogee (Creek) Nation, by the Deep Fork of the Canadian River. The library and archives had lists segregating "by blood" tribal members from freedmen and freedwomen for all five nations. Although no Cades appeared on the rolls I saw, there were Turners, Reeves, and Allens. But were any of them *my* Turners,

Reeves, or Allens? Without more than surnames, it was impossible to learn if any rolls listed my mother's ancestors, by blood or not.

What I did learn was that the Cherokee Nation had revoked tribal citizenship of descendants of its freedmen and women. A knoll overlooking Tahlequah, capital of the nation, still goes by the name "Nigger Hill."

. . .

Before leaving Oklahoma I returned to flowing water, crossing the Cimarron River—its ripples aglint and aglitter in slant waning light. *Cimarron*—wild, untamed—is a good name. Centuries earlier *los cimarrónes* had escaped Spanish slavery to live in seclusion on the isthmus of Central America.

Wading into the river's insistent flow I could almost believe the impulse of life. At a confluence these waters merged with another channel's flow, their sand and mud loads merging, too. Many rivers become one in Oklahoma, but not human beings or blood streams.

Bridging the distance between history and the particularities of family seemed an impossible task given the erosive and estranging power displacement could wield. Circumstances leaving no trace could outweigh any longing to remain in a homeplace. Any continuity forged by knowing one's lineages of kinship could break and break.

The river surface blushed in the last crimson light of day. Perhaps, I thought, wounds also flow in the blood. As if rending could begin in one's veins and arteries, leaving partial access but never the whole. Self-knowledge reworked over generations becoming piecework.

But *piecework* needn't mean empty. *Fragmented* needn't mean all gone. Ankle-deep in the Cimarron, I needed to believe this.

*

SILENCE CAN BE a sanctuary or frame for stories told. Silence also obscures origins. My parents' muteness once seemed tacit consent that generational history was no longer part of life or living memory. That a past survived was best left unexposed or even forgotten as self-defense. But unvoiced lives cut a sharp-felt absence. Neither school lessons nor images surging around me could offer salve or substitute. My greatest fear as a young girl was that I wasn't meant to exist.

Yet one idea stood firm: The American land preceded hate. My child-sense of its antiquity became as much a refuge as any place, whether the Devil's Punchbowl or a canyon called Grand. Still, silences embedded in a family, and in a society, couldn't be replaced even by sounds so reliable: of water spilling down rock, of a thunderstorm rolling into far distance, or of branches sifting wind.

By the end of the nineteenth century some of my mother's people had left rural Alabama and Virginia behind for the capital of Pennsylvania. How or if Oklahoma entered, or what existed before plantations, I don't yet know. Scattered elements of language, like Momma's Pennsylvania *thee*, touch me. Dad's forebears took different paths, known and unknown, through the Chesapeake tidewater and Piedmont. Choices both parents made cast long shadows over me. The unvoiced history of this continent calls, too. It may ground all.

An immense land lies about us. Nations migrate within us. The past looms close, as immediate as breath, blood, and scars on a wrist. It, too, lies hidden, obscured, shattered. What I can know of ancestors' lives or of this land can't be retrieved like old postcards stored in a desk drawer. To *re-member* is to know that traces now without name, like the "unidentified" subjects in O. E. Aultman's photographs, still mark a very real presence. To *re-member* is to discover patterns in fragments. As an Earth historian I once sought the relics of deep time. To be an honest woman, I must trace other residues of hardness.

Far from any real town, my house sits at the edge of a field cleared two centuries ago, bordered by relict stone walls and wooded, worn-down hills. So different from the Devil's Punchbowl or Cimarron plains, this landscape is yet kin and reminder. I like to walk through hemlock, white pine, and hardwood cover to the top of Long Hill, the ancient rocky mass behind my home. It's on rain-soaking walks especially, when drops strike exposed schist, that tracing hardness seems most necessary.

ALIEN LAND ETHIC:
THE DISTANCE BETWEEN

When I was a horse, a wild Appaloosa full of speed, I'd run up and down sidewalks, around playgrounds and our yard—just to feel wind rush with me. But once the world moved beyond sense, I began to run from what I feared. Riots near our new home in Washington, D.C., left burnt, gutted remains of buildings I knew. The "war" in Vietnam joined us at dinner each night as TV footage of wounded soldiers, of crying women and children, of places with names like Khe Sanh, My Lai. Assassinations of men my parents called "good men" meant anyone—my parents, my friends, or I—could disappear at any time. Even the familiar *Good night, Chet. Good night, David, and good night for NBC News* no longer comforted.

I learned by the age of eight that hate could be spit wetting the front of my favorite, mom-made dress. Hate could be a classmate's sing-song "never saw nothin' as ugly as a *nigger*, never saw nothin' as crummy as a *nigger*." His eyes on me.

I ran not just to feel wind, but in hope it would blow away whatever it was about me that was bad and hate-deserving. Safety lived in my room, in my mother's arms, and outdoors on a land that never judged or spat.

Does your child-mind haunt you, too?

Confusing doubts pushed and pulled. Whether vestigial or preparative they held on. I donned silent passivity as armor—and avoided mirrors. Only teenage encounters with writings by authors who also seemed to be searching prompted me to speak. I met them question to question.

THE SISTERS OF Providence and lay teachers of Immaculata Preparatory School assigned four summer readings to my section of the entering ninth-grade class. They'd be part of the coming year's courses. Although the fourth book is lost to memory, the other three—*Man's Search for Meaning* by Viktor Frankl, *The Heart Is a Lonely Hunter* by Carson McCullers, and *A Sand County Almanac and Sketches Here and There* by Aldo Leopold—struck me deeply. The worn copies still sit on my shelves within easy reach.

A Sand County Almanac was published in the autumn of 1949, more than a year after Leopold's death. That his work was hailed as landmark or, in Wallace Stegner's words, "a famous, almost holy book in conservation circles," I knew nothing about. Nor did I know that this forester, wildlife manager, educator, conservation leader, and writer born in Iowa in 1887 was called by some a "prophet." What appealed to my fourteen-year-old sensibilities were the intimate images of land and seasons in place: an atom's recycling odyssey through time; the chickadee, "so small a bundle of large enthusiasms"; the crane's call "the trumpet in the orchestra of evolution." And my favorite passage, from "Song of the Gavilan":

This song of the waters is audible to every ear, but there is other music in these hills, by no means audible to all. To hear even a few notes of it you must first live here for a long time, and you must know the speech of hills and rivers. Then on a still night, when the campfire is low and the Pleiades have climbed over rimrocks, sit quietly and listen for a wolf to howl, and think hard of everything you have seen and tried to understand. Then

you may hear it—a vast pulsing harmony—its score inscribed
on a thousand hills, its notes the lives and deaths of plants and
animals, its rhythms spanning the seconds and the centuries.

What also appealed was the seeming openness of this man's
struggle to frame a personal truth. In "The Land Ethic," Aldo Leopold enlarged the boundaries of "community" to include "soils,
waters, plants, and animals, or collectively: the land." Though I
couldn't find words then, his call for an extension of ethics to land
relations seemed to express a sense of responsibility and reciprocity
not yet embraced by this country but embedded in many Indigenous peoples' traditions of experience—that land is fully inhabited,
intimate with immediate presence.

These ideas prompted new questions. If, as Mr. Leopold wrote,
"obligations have no meaning without conscience, and the problem
we face is the extension of the social conscience from people to
land," then what part of this nation still lacked conscience broad
enough to realize the internal change of mind and heart, to embrace "evolutionary possibility" and "ecological necessity"? Why
was it that human relations in the United States I knew at age fourteen could be so cruel?

Other passages in *A Sand County Almanac* confused: "The era-
sure of a human subspecies is largely painless—to us—if we know
little enough about it. A dead Chinaman is of little import to us
whose awareness of things Chinese is bounded by an occasional
dish of chow mein. We grieve only for what we know." Why not
know "things Chinese"?

I couldn't understand why, in a book so concerned with America's past, the only reference to slavery, to human beings as property,
was about ancient Greece.

What I wanted more than anything was to speak with Mr.
Leopold. To ask him. I so feared that his "we" and "us" excluded

me and other Americans with ancestral roots in Africa, Asia, or Native America. Only uncertainty and estrangement felt within my teenage reach.

Did Aldo Leopold consider me?

JULY 8TH. THE initial phone interview went well, so well my prospective employer wanted to meet in person that afternoon just as a formality. A collector and trader of Civil War memorabilia, he'd advertised in *The Washington Post* for a summer assistant to help him catalogue and work at fairs. He sounded impressed that a young teenager knew details of the war's campaigns, of the landscapes where battles took place. I remember my excitement, wearing my most grown-up dress, crossing the Potomac River to Virginia that steamy day; ascending the steps of an old Alexandria row house, knocking. I remember the heavy door opening, my practiced "Hello, I'm Lauret Savoy," and his single word as the door closed. *Sorry.*

I don't remember: How long I stood on those steps. The ride home. Why I watched an ancient rerun of *The Mickey Mouse Club*, singing along with Annette, Darlene, and the other pale mouseketeers.

My mother came home early that afternoon from her nursing job at Howard University Hospital. What could I tell her? But as she entered the living room, flanked and supported by two of her co-workers, a voice spoke out: *Your father died this afternoon.* Momma later told me that he was found in his ward room holding the telephone.

Dad had been in and out of the hospital many times that last year, dying shortly after learning cancer had spread from lung to bone, two months shy of his sixtieth birthday. He and I spoke little in that time. There seemed little to say, as if silence itself could metastasize between a man who expected much, and was often disappointed, and his only child who thought his only words to her were *Think* and *Use your brain.*

Born September 1916 in Washington, D.C., to Laura Wilson Savoy and Alfred Kiger Savoy, a principal and later assistant superintendent of the District's "colored" public schools, Willard Wilson Savoy grew to be a man who in appearance would be accepted without question by those calling themselves "white." Pale of complexion with gray-blue eyes, he'd not be seen or treated as other until he admitted "Negro" blood.

A memory: We are walking hand-in-hand on a Los Angeles sidewalk one bright afternoon and pass an acquaintance of his. I'm four or five years old and catch the emphasis in the question asked. "This is your daughter?"

Years before meeting my mother and more than a decade before my birth, my father had a novel published. The year was 1949. After serving in the segregated Army Air Forces during the Second World War, he wrote about an embittered "mulatto" boy-becomes-man who thinks he might escape prejudice, and his own demons, by redefining himself as white. The book's title: *Alien Land.*

But I knew none of this, not until I stumbled upon the book late one night in the basement stacks of my university library. It was the end of my first year there. The dedication alone convinced me of a chance for dialogue after death: "To the child which my wife and I may someday have—and to the children of each American—in the fervent hope that at least one shall be brought to see more clearly the enduring need for simple humanity."

Yes, I stole the book, last checked out years earlier. Yes, I ran from it many times. Kern, the boy-becomes-man, and I shared too many experiences of hurt, too many questions.

A little boy's wondering:

A question that had become centered around that part of the pledge that said, "—one Nation, indivisible, with liberty and justice for all." . . . Kern had for some time entertained doubts that liberty and justice were "—for all." "Jim Crow" in Washington, the Capital of the Nation, did not seem to him to be "liberty and justice for all." But then, he supposed such things were written into the Constitution and Bill of Rights just for white boys and girls.

An eleven-year-old's experience:

He listened intently as Frank Richards talked about subscribers and gave him advice about setting up his route. "—keep your territory compact—" . . .

"Guess we can start you with fifty copies. Think you can get rid of them?" Kern nodded happily. "You'll get three and a half cents for each copy you sell—"

Kern busied himself with the arithmetic of three and one half times fifty. One dollar and seventy-five cents! The total surprised him. Almost two dollars a week. He began to plan what he would do with it.

"Where do you live—uh—Kern?" Kern answered, his eyes still on a picture booklet showing a model Scott Home Salesman standing at a door, hat in hand, as he talked to a customer. He did not notice that Frank Richards had stopped writing.

"You mean North*east*, don't you?" He had looked up at Kern.

"No sir, I mean—" Kern realized what the man meant. "I mean Northwest." He held tightly to the booklet and hoped it wouldn't happen.

Sick and suddenly miserable, inside, he hoped it wouldn't happen.

It did.

"I thought white folks had all moved out from there—"

"They ha—" Kern cut himself off. Too late now to cut himself off—to say that a few families still lived there.

"What are you, boy?" Frank Richards dropped his pen on the desk and turned in his chair to face Kern. Kern looked back at him, saying nothing.

"You a white boy?"

Kern shook his head slowly. "No."

Richards reached forward and drew Kern's hand roughly toward the lamp on the desk. He started at the outstretched fingers.

"Blue nails! 'Course you ain't white. A nigger! Well, I'll be damned!" He stood up and took Kern by the shoulder. "Come on, boy," he led him through the hall and out to the porch.

"Get on . . . I ain't doin' no business with no niggers."

That night, after the house was dark, after even the chirping of the crickets had dropped to silence, Kern lay on his bed, wide awake, staring at the ceiling.

"Why?"

The question pulsed in him. Sickness. Anger. Shame. None of these answered the question. He got up and turned on his desk lamp. Then he stood in front of the mirror and stared at his face. . . . Stared at his eyes. They were blue. His nose was lean and his mouth was thin and straight.

"Why? Why am I a nigger?"

His fingers went along the tracery of veins at his temples, dull blue under the skin. He turned and bent under the lamp to peer closely at his fingers. They were not blue. They were pink. Pink except for the little half-moon at the top of each nail. And those were white. His thought became words in the room.

"Why am I a nigger?"

My father's "alien land" grew from the "hypocrisy which, in one breath preached the doctrine that all men were created free and equal and, in the very next breath, denied to millions the simple respect which should naturally go with such a belief."

I understood then that I, too, lived in an alien land. A fourteen-year-old's questions became an eighteen-year-old's need to understand why such hypocrisy and inhumanity continued. Why my father never told me about this book, or about the wounds and scar tissue of his own growing up. About how he survived not "passing."

Partial answer to the first "why" came soon enough in Ashley Montagu's course on the fallacy of race, but it wasn't answer enough. How was I to survive? I couldn't "pass" as Kern could. Besides, I wasn't sure I wanted to. I hoped instead that safety would come from my fading into the background, unnoticed.

alien. land. ethic. Three words published midway through a century of world wars—as a young man's semi-autobiographical novel, and as "The Land Ethic," climax essay in an older man's "end-result of a lifetime journey." What happened in the postwar years while my father and Aldo Leopold wrote and revised?

U.S. immigration quotas continue to favor those from northwestern Europe while severely restricting entry from Africa, Asia, the Pacific Islands, southern and eastern Europe. Hiroshima and Nagasaki, devastated by the first practical use of uranium and plutonium bombs, begin to recover. Nearly 120,000 Japanese Americans who'd been confined in remote internment camps for three years under Executive Order 9066 try to rebuild their lives—about two-thirds of them citizens, the Nisei or those born in the United States to immigrant parents. Survivors of Nazi concentration camps search for home. The president of General Electric suggests "a permanent war economy," while a business magazine reports that President Truman's policies assure "maintaining and building our preparations for war will be big business in the United States for at least a considerable period ahead." Archibald MacLeish, then assistant secretary of state, reflects on these years: "As things are now going, the peace we will make, the peace we seem to be making, will be a peace of oil, a peace of gold, a peace of shipping, a peace, in brief . . . without moral purpose or human interest."

What else? The United States chooses not to ratify UNESCO's Universal Declaration of Human Rights, a document Eleanor Roosevelt believed would "establish standards for human rights and freedom the world over." The nation's capital, my father's home, remains a segregated city. Even Red Cross blood is segregated. (Dr. Charles Drew, the African American physician who developed the blood bank—and a surgeon who worked with my mother at Freedman's Hospital—had been fired from his job of coordinating wartime donations when he tried to end this government-approved policy.) And, in this decade, at least thirty-three persons, nearly all African Americans, are lynched.

Both Aldo Leopold and my father offered telling visions of American life at midcentury. *A Sand County Almanac* and *Alien Land* are inseparable in my thinking. Yet who else, then or now, would put these books on the same shelf?

. . .

After Odysseus returned home, the aged nurse Eurycleia informed him that a dozen of his serving women had misbehaved during his long absence, having slept with Penelope's suitors. Odysseus hanged them. Leopold began "The Land Ethic" with a reference to the "slave-girls" in Homer's *Odyssey*, noting that the "ethical structure of that day . . . had not yet been extended to human chattels." He continued:

> An ethic, ecologically, is a limitation on freedom of action in the struggle for existence. An ethic, philosophically, is a differentiation of social from anti-social conduct. These are two definitions of one thing. The thing has its origin in the tendency of interdependent individuals or groups to evolve modes of co-operation. The ecologist calls these symbioses. Politics and economics are advanced symbioses in which the original free-for-all competition has been replaced, in part, by co-operative mechanisms with an ethical content. . . .
>
> There is as yet no ethic dealing with man's relation to land and to the animals and plants which grow upon it. Land, like Odysseus' slave-girls, is still property. The land-relation is strictly economic, entailing privileges but not obligations.

Leopold added that an ethic could be regarded "as a mode of guidance for meeting ecological situations so new or intricate, or involving such deferred reactions, that the path of social expediency is not discernible to the average individual." As "a kind of community instinct in-the-making," ethics rested on the premise "that the individual is a member of a community of interdependent parts" now enlarged to include the land. Then: "This sounds simple: do we not already sing our love for and obligation to the land of the free and the home of the brave? Yes, but just what and whom do we love?"

At fourteen I wondered who, exactly, "we" are. I wondered, too, what and whom "we" love. Neither an equality of interdependence nor an evenness of cooperation seemed to underlie this country's human relations. Not in the internment of Japanese Americans just seven years before Leopold's and my father's books appeared. Nor in the de facto and de jure segregation that so many Americans took for granted as the second half of the twentieth century began.

If viewed as a trophic or food strategy, one group of people acting upon another by imposing values, definitions, or violence could be seen as deriving part of its energy by consuming or controlling the energies of others. Or so I thought in an ecology course where definitions of parasitism and predator-prey dynamics seemed disturbingly close to some human relations.

Calling morality prescriptive rather than descriptive of behavior, one commentary on Leopold's land ethic argued that "moral consciousness is expanding more rapidly now than ever before." Despite continued failings in moral practice, the author cited as evidence emergent moral ideals like civil rights, human rights, and women's liberation. "Most educated people today," he added, "pay lip service at least to the ethical precept that all members of the human species, regardless of race, creed, or national origin, are endowed with certain fundamental rights which it is wrong not to respect." Well-meaning acquaintances have also told me that civil rights laws and a growing attention to human rights now address root causes of human ills. They've suggested that racism, class conflict, sexism, homophobia, and xenophobia could well become isolated aberrations or vestiges of the way things used to be. Just as slavery, dispossession, and internment became things of the past, they say, so can these. "Don't you know we're becoming a post-racial society?"

What have I missed?

Perhaps the sphere of ethical relevancy has expanded outward among "educated people" to embrace race, gender, and class in theory if not practice. But who lives in theory, or benefits from lip service? Without backing belief or means, "rights" become limited and limiting to legal form and process rather than a moral imperative extending from heart and spirit. It still matters to me that more than three score years after the Supreme Court ruled segregation in American public schools unconstitutional, separate and *un*equal education remains the embedded norm.

A great many things have changed since 1949. Much has not.

With origins from all parts of the world, "we the people" inherit and share the contradictions of this nation's growth. We carry this history within us, the past becoming present in what we think and do, in who we think we are. It informs our senses of place on Earth and our ties with each other.

A child born today enters a world of rapid and extensive change. The list is often repeated: Human population continues to grow. Ecosystems around the world have never before been so fragmented or degraded, resulting in great losses to the diversity of life. Coal, petroleum, and other fossil hydrocarbons, once abundant and seemingly cheap "resources," literally fueled industrial revolutions and the mechanization of food production. And because of this fossil-fuel economy, greenhouse gas levels continue to climb, exceeding the highest atmospheric concentrations since our species evolved.

The pace and degree of such environmental changes are unprecedented in human history. Yet the embedded systems and norms behind them in the United States, the most energy-consumptive nation, are not. Their deep roots allowed and continue to amplify fragmented ways of seeing, valuing, and using nature, as well as human beings.

Consider the "ecological footprint." Its estimate can mask how exploitations of land and of people are intertwined. Quantifying the area of productive land and water needed to provide ecosystem "services" or resources that are used (like clean water, food, fuel), and wastes then generated, gives but a partial measure of the biosphere's regenerative capacity. And by this measure alone humanity's footprint already exceeds Earth's ecological limits.

But American prosperity and progress have come at great human costs, too. Forced removals of the continent's Native peoples yielded land to newcomers from Europe and their descendants. The new republic's economy grew upon a foundation of industrial agriculture built and powered by enslaved workers. Consuming *other* people's labor, dispossessing *other* people of land and life connection to it, devaluing human rights, and diminishing one's community, autonomy, and health—these are not just events of the past. In a globalizing world, American agribusiness giants have profited from the products of enslaved labor in Brazil at a seemingly safe moral distance. And far too many degraded environments in the United States are also citizens' homes—in nearly all states with hazardous waste facilities, high percentages of people of color and the economically poor live, and die, next to those sites. Witness, too, farm workers in pesticide-laden fields whose health and lives are rarely recognized as a cost of producing cheap food.

A wiser measure of the ecological footprint would include people, or at least their labor. It might factor in the losses of relationships with land or home, losses of self-determination, and losses of health or life. What if the footprint measured, over time, on whom and what the nation's foot has trod—that is, who has paid for prosperity?

ALIEN LAND. LAND ethic. What is the distance between them? As a young adult I felt little integrity or wholeness of living because so much of my acquired knowledge came from inculcated divisions. Only slowly did I come to see that I would remain complicit in my own diminishment unless I stepped out of the *separate* trap: me from you, us from them, brown skin from depigmented skin, relations among people from relations with the land.

Aldo Leopold explained, in *A Sand County Almanac*, that he "purposely presented the land ethic as a product of social evolution because nothing so important as an ethic is ever 'written.'"

Rather than being fixed, an ethic must evolve "in the minds of a thinking community." As he wrote toward his tentative expression of possibility and necessity, Leopold was concerned not just about the primacy of utilitarian values in the United States, but also the inadequacies of dis-integrated thinking and living. Specialization encouraged fragmented recordings and understandings of human experience. He worried as well that the goals and definitions of science dealt "almost exclusively with the creation and exercise of power." An unfinished manuscript and notes, published posthumously as the essay "Conservation," offer his developing insights: "We shall never achieve harmony with land, any more than we shall achieve justice or liberty for people. In these higher aspirations the important thing is not to achieve, but to strive."

The scope of America's "thinking community" remains narrow. A democratic dream of individual liberties and rights hasn't yet contributed to a "co-ordinated whole"—whether human, biotic, or the land. Danger lies in equating theory with practice, or ideal with committed action, as personal responsibility and respect for others, and for the land, can still be lost to lip service, disingenuous manners, and legislated gestures to an ideal.

Consider the words of a biologist writing on an environmental ethic today. "Our troubles," E. O. Wilson observes in *The Diversity of Life*, "arise from the fact that we do not know what we are and cannot agree on what we want to be. The primary cause of this intellectual failure is ignorance of our origins." "Humanity is part of nature," he continues, "a species that evolved among other species. The more closely we identify ourselves with the rest of life, the more quickly we will be able to discover the sources of human sensibility and acquire the knowledge on which an enduring ethic, a sense of preferred direction, can be built." Perhaps danger lies most basically in not recognizing who and what *we* are.

• • •

pored through my father's shelves after reading *Alien Land* that first year at Princeton, concentrating on books he'd marked. *On Being Negro in America. Black Skin, White Masks. The Fire Next Time. Anger, and Beyond.* These writings showed me that no question, no fear, no anger or shame was unique to me or my time. Still, all of it was achingly personal to each writer. I remember drawing slight comfort in knowing others before me had shared doubt, confusion, or worse. I also recall what at first seemed a bottomless fear-fright once I realized the vicious persistence of human ugliness.

Not long ago I came upon an old box of words my father had packed and sealed before his death. Stacked within it were brittle and yellowed novel manuscripts, journals, decades of letters and photographs, and this newspaper clipping of an ad he had placed:

Monday, March 2, 1959
San Francisco Chronicle

WANTED TO RENT

NEGRO Account Executive and
published novelist; wife, operating room
supervisor, wish to live as human beings
in San Francisco. Seek unprejudiced
landlord to make desirable apt. rental
without regard to race. QUIET IS ALL
IMPORTANT. Need 3 to 4 rooms plus
modern kitchen, bath, minimum 9-12 mo.
lease in $100 mo. range. Call OL3-8242,
10 a.m. to 7:30 p.m.

I've long wondered what a child inherits from a parent, within and beyond the strain of blood—and beyond bitterness and silence lining adolescent memories. Did I overhear or imagine Dad say how he hated the America that believed its lies?

Another ninth-grade summer text was *Man's Search for Meaning* by Viktor Frankl, a survivor of Auschwitz and other Nazi camps who became a leading psychiatrist in postwar Europe. I became obsessed by the last two sentences of his 1959 book: "Our generation is realistic, for we have come to know man as he really is. After all, man is that being who has invented the gas chambers of Auschwitz; however, he is also that being who has entered those gas chambers upright, with the Lord's Prayer or the *Shema Yisrael* on his lips." Frankl believed that "each man is questioned by life; and he can only answer to life by *answering for* his own life; to life he can only respond by being responsible." He added that "everything can be taken from a man but one thing: the last of the human freedoms—to choose one's attitude in any given set of circumstances, to choose one's own way" and thus "evoke his will to meaning from its state of latency."

What did Frankl's words of choice mean for an adolescent, for her generation? Could one choose between ignorance and innocence in such a world? In the passing years I began to doubt any emergence from a "state of latency," doubted whether Americans as a whole could choose to answer these questions broadly: What and whom do you love and respect? To what and whom are you responsible, obligated? Respect, from the Latin *respicere*, the willingness to look again. Responsibility, the ability to respond, the capacity to attend, to stand behind one's acts. Conscience, from the Latin *conscientia*, a joint knowledge or feeling, from *conscire* (*com-*, together with, and *scire*, to know). If obligations have no meaning without conscience, without an acceptance of moral responsibility, what is possible?

Fourteen years before *A Sand County Almanac* and *Alien Land* went to print, in a decade defined by the Depression and the Dust

Bowl, Aldo Leopold and his family began to restore abandoned, "worn out" farmland along the Wisconsin River near Baraboo. They planted native prairie grasses, wildflowers, shrubs and, eventually, many thousands of trees. This was the sand county whose seasonal cycles of life and death the "almanac" celebrated. This was land that felt both familiar and welcoming one recent October dawn, when I took a worn path to that river's edge to watch the sun rise over the downstream horizon. The gift of time by these waters came from the Aldo Leopold Foundation. On the Wisconsin River's sand plain, a fourteen-year-old's questions met the clearest-yet responses.

I could imagine it possible to refrain from dis-integrated thinking and living, from a fragmented understanding of human experience on this continent. Possible to refuse what alienates and separates. To see in fugitive pieces the forces that have shaped the land and ourselves in it. Of course, there is always a danger of fooling myself. But if it is possible, then perhaps a larger sense of who we are as interconnected ecological, cultural, and historical beings could begin to grow. For if the health of the land is its capacity for self-renewal, then the health of the human family could, in part, be an intergenerational capacity for locating ourselves within many inheritances: as citizens of the land, of nations even within a nation, and of Earth. Democracy lies within ever widening communities.

Questioned by life we are held to account. Aldo Leopold and my father never met in their lifetimes. I want *alien land* and *land ethic* to meet and answer to each other in ours.

Postscript

There will be many readers who will be contented with the charming nature vignettes and the attractive illustrations, closing [*A Sand County Almanac*] hurriedly when they discover the knotty philosophical problem in the last part. That will be a pity, for these ideas were the man's life, and because of them we can place this book on the shelf that holds the writings of Thoreau and John Muir.

—J. W. H., *San Francisco Chronicle* (November 27, 1949)

Alien Land, by Willard Savoy . . . is written with passion and with anger, so that it has a vitality which makes it linger in the mind. Reduced to its simplest terms it is the story of a man's loss of the sense of personal dignity, a loss that began in his childhood, continued through his adolescence, and into manhood; and of how he struggled to regain it.

—Ann Petry, *The Saturday Review* (April 30, 1949)

MADELINE TRACES

Many headwaters rise in the midcontinent. They flow as the terrain suggests, toward the Mississippi River, toward Hudson Bay, toward the great lake named Superior. Here the forty-ninth parallel's smooth line separating western provinces from western states becomes a rougher border, its irregularity determined by the lay of land and water. A visitor to the boreal woodlands and lakes of northern Wisconsin and Minnesota might suspect that time moves slowly here. But anyone equating gentle topography with quietness does so at great peril. Tumultuous histories lie beneath subtle appearances. They have a far reach.

A friend's gift of solitude brought me to Lake Superior's southwestern shore, to her cottage on Madeline Island, largest of the Apostle Islands. On leave from my job, I wanted to spend the turn of summer to fall in a quiet space, sifting contents of a large box I'd recently found, the box my father had packed and sealed before his death decades ago. I was a child when he taped the box shut. I was barely an adolescent when he died. Releasing its contents wouldn't be a simple act.

From Penny's cottage and its fronting beach on the island's northern shore, the horizon sweeps west to north. From here one can track the sun's apparent movement southward into autumn and preview the coming of weather from great distance. For weeks I traced the passage of storms and a season, learning to distinguish wind sifted by white pine from wind in red pine and birch. Always each day ended on the beach. I liked to sit among the cobbles of basalt, granite, and layered sandstone, a strandline clutch of red and black lithic eggs. Beyond, lake merged with sky.

I'd never before visited the Apostle Islands or northwestern Wisconsin and assumed my ignorance of the region's human history, of its landscapes and layers of names, meant little if anything here connected to me. Madeline Island would simply be where I entered my father's box. But as I came to be *in* this place, came to learn names and stories both born and put here, my mistake became clear. Even grade-school wanderings through history, literature, and science began to show a much darker side.

I take many lessons from Madeline Island. One is this: I am both a collector and an arrangement. I might gather stones, collect books, or save mementos. But my own experiences, too, are gathered up and swept along by currents of a still-unfolding history on this vast continent. This northland touched me as a child and knows me still. Though I was unaware, its own life included mine. I suspect it might include yours, too.

• • •

Kitchigame Kitchi-gumi Geetche-gumi Lake Superior

Moningwanekaning Moningwanaykaning Madeline Island

Anishinaabe Ojibwe Ojibway Chippewa

In *Names on the Land*, George R. Stewart recounts that French voyageurs traveling by canoe came to a lake so large they at first called it Mer Douce, or Freshwater Sea, later referring to it as Lake of the Hurons. These men had also heard of another lake upstream, which they named "Lac Supérieur, 'Upper Lake' as if only two lakes were concerned." The English then used that name without translating it. They presumed a different meaning: "Lake Superior," one wrote, "is so called on account of its being superior in magnitude to any of the lakes on that vast continent.'"

Waterways and woodlands encountered by the French and English weren't nameless. The uppermost and largest of the string of Great Lakes had long been known to the Anishinaabe as Kitchigame, the great inland sea. Gerald Vizenor, author and a descendant of these original people of the woodland lakes, remembers Madeline Island as "our tribal home, the place where the earth began, the place that first came back from the flood. Naanabozho, the trickster, was born here, on this island; the old men told us he was the first little person in the world. He stole fire from across the lake. We are little people. This is our place on the earth, this place is in our bodies, in our words and in our dreams." This home, Moningwanekaning in Anishinaabemowin, is the island of the golden-breasted woodpecker. Kechenezuhyauh, the first recorded leader of the Anishinaabe crane clan, lived on Madeline Island in the seventeenth century. Vizenor, a crane descendant on his father's side, describes how "people measured life in the circles of the sun and moon and human heart. Trailing the summer shores of *kitchigame* to the hardwoods and maple sugar swamps and stands of *manomin*—wild rice—many families of the *anishinabe* returned each winter to *moningwanekaning* and told stories of the summer past."

The Anishinaabe did not name themselves Ojibwa or Chippewa. *Ojibwa* was invented by Henry Rowe Schoolcraft, an Anglo-American remembered in elementary and secondary schoolbooks as an early expert on the land's Indigenous peoples. By one account the word *Ojibwa* was misheard and recorded into nineteenth-century treaties between the federal government and Anishinaabe as "Chippewa." An invention and a mistake became official names. Vizenor has lamented that the *"anishinabe* must still wear the invented names. The tragedy is that today many young *oshki anishinabe* do not know the difference between the names."

Lake Superior is Kitchigame, the great freshwater sea of the Anishinaabe. Madeline Island is Moningwanekaning. The Anishinaabe were called Ojibwa and Chippewa by strangers.

THAT HENRY ROWE Schoolcraft was a stranger seemed to matter little to those keeping paper records. Charles McCullough, a founder of the Canadian Club movement, referred to him to as "a highly versatile man. He was a well-grounded geologist, an authority on American ethnology and archaeology, a much-travelled explorer-geographer, an historian, journalist, editor and poet withal. He was a true friend of the Indians and won their esteem and confidence." This highly versatile man is the Schoolcraft introduced to me in fifth-grade social studies as the discoverer of the Mississippi River's source and leading "Indian scholar" of his day. So enthralled was I by this apparently intrepid explorer of both wild lands and Native peoples that I chose Schoolcraft's work and life as the topic of my class report. I learned and recounted "facts" available to me through my basic library skills:

1. Henry Rowe Schoolcraft was born in 1793 near Albany, New York, and died in 1864 in Washington, D.C.
2. In 1817 he traveled to the Mississippi Valley and later published his observations. They were praised as a detailed and reliable study of the region's minerals.
3. Secretary of War John C. Calhoun appointed Schoolcraft to the 1820 expedition in Michigan Territory to verify rumors of copper riches. His reports were the first published accounts of mineral wealth around Lake Superior.

They helped spur both mining and geologic study, thus aiding the nation's economic foundation and the growth of scientific knowledge.

4. In 1822 Secretary Calhoun appointed Schoolcraft an Indian agent in the Michigan Territory. He lived with prominent trader John Johnston; his wife, a daughter of an Ojibwa or Chippewa leader; and their children. In 1823 Schoolcraft married the Johnstons' daughter Jane.

5. In 1832 Schoolcraft discovered the source of the Mississippi River, which he named Lake Itasca by combining syllables from the Latin words *veritas caput* for "true source."

6. Lewis Cass, then governor of the Michigan Territory, wanted to know more about the different tribal people living there. Prompted by Cass's questions—such as "Do they relate stories, or indulge in any works of the imagination?"—Schoolcraft sought Chippewa stories. With the help of his Johnston in-laws he began to collect them.

7. As the first American to gather and publish Indian stories in nearly original form, Schoolcraft became the "father" of American folklore and anthropology. His first large work, published in 1839, was *Algic Researches, Comprising Inquiries Respecting the Mental Characteristics of the North American Indians, First Series: Indian Tales and Legends.*

8. The great poet Henry Wadsworth Longfellow based his masterpiece *The Song of Hiawatha* on tales he read in *Algic Researches.*

Henry Rowe Schoolcraft the explorer, Indian agent, geologist, and anthropologist was a quintessential American hero in this simple, unquestioned sequence of events. As a ten-year-old I didn't recognize any complexity or contradiction in the man's life or work; I simply retrieved, accepted, and repeated printed stories. The man was born.

He lived, doing X, Y, and Z, nearly all of them praiseworthy achievements. He died, leaving a legacy to science and literature. End of (a great) story. Besides, no other perspectives appeared to exist.

Not only was I unaware that narratives of the past aren't simply actual events recounted under the authority of truth, I'd also adopted a perspective along with its weighty baggage of assumptions and attitudes. Of conflicting points of view or contending interests my ignorance was nearly complete. That Schoolcraft's geographic "discovery" came from his asking Native peoples the location of the river's source. That as "Indian agent" and geologist, he helped the federal government claim and redefine the land around Lake Superior as a controlled target of mining through treaty cessions from the Anishinaabe. That this man, first married to a young "mixedblood" Anishinaabe woman, later married a woman who in her own words was "so satisfied that slavery is the school God has established for the conversion of barbarous nations." That this frontier anthropologist renamed and categorized the Anishinaabe. And that this early scholar of "American Indian folklore" had an eye toward literary markets and reworked living oral narratives into static specimens to be sold.

"The man, it may be, shall pass away from the earth, but these tributes to the best feelings of the heart will remain, while these simple tales and legendary creations constitute a new point of character by which he should be judged. They are, at least, calculated to modify our views of the man, who is not always a savage, not always a fiend." What would I have understood had I, at ten, read these elegiac words in the introduction to Schoolcraft's *The Myth of Hiawatha and Other Oral Legends, Mythologic and Allegoric, of the North American Indians*, published in 1856? I already greatly admired the "myth" from having learned Henry Wadsworth Longfellow's poem at age seven.

I still recall the weeks spent memorizing lines, each second grader with a part in our class production of *The Song of Hiawatha*.

When the day came—our desks arranged in a circle around the classroom to leave a center stage—the *thump-thump-thumping* on our teacher's drum signaling us to begin:

By the shores of Gitche Gumee,	(The first of *my* lines)
By the shining Big-Sea-Water	(my arms and hands move as ripples on water)
Stood the wigwam of Nokomis	(arms extend overhead, my fingertips touch)
Daughter of the Moon, Nokomis . . .	(my arms reach out to the sky . . .)

This child-memory remains intact, still full of innocence and dearness. I was proud and deeply moved to know a *real* Indian story.

Longfellow's book-length poem received great acclaim on its publication in 1855, immediately selling out its first printing. In that edition, Longfellow explained:

> This Indian Edda—if I may so call it—is founded on a tradition, prevalent among the North American Indians, of a personage of miraculous birth, who was sent among them to clear their rivers, forests, and fishing-grounds, and to teach them the arts of peace. He was known among different tribes by the several names. . . . Into this old tradition I have woven other curious Indian legends, drawn chiefly from the various and valuable writings of Mr. Schoolcraft, to whom the literary world is greatly indebted for his indefatigable zeal in rescuing from oblivion so much of the legendary lore of the Indians.
>
> The scene of the poem is among the Ojibways on the southern shore of Lake Superior . . .

As Hiawatha prepares to leave his people at poem's end, he advises them to give up their old ways and embrace the ways of the "Black-Robe chief, the Pale-face":

> I am going, O my people,
> On a long and distant journey . . .
> But my guests I leave behind me;
> Listen to their words of wisdom,
> Listen to the truth they tell you,
> For the Master of Life has sent them,
> From the land of light and morning!

Longfellow might have viewed *The Song of Hiawatha* as a poetic restating of tribal voices and traditions, but he borrowed, distorted, and invented. Many have since noticed that the relentless, pulsing trochaic meter that so moved the child-me resembles that of the Finnish epic poem *Kalevala*. While the stories came mainly from Schoolcraft's *Algic Researches*, Longfellow was accused of borrowing a few incidents from *Kalevala*. He even changed names. Schoolcraft recalled "the myth of the Indians of a remarkable personage, who is called Manabozho by the Algonquins, and Hiawatha by the Iroquois, who was the instructor of the tribes in arts and knowledge, was first related to me in 1822, by Chippewas of Lake Superior." Longfellow preferred Hiawatha: "I chose it instead of Manabozho (Ojibway) for the sake of euphony."

Schoolcraft even suggested that the poem's "theme of native lore reveals one of the true sources of our literary independence" from Europe. He didn't seem troubled that such American literary "independence" came from an invented "Indian" voice that dislocated and rendered complex traditions into simplistic forms.

The Song of Hiawatha eventually found its way into dozens of languages. To me what is most telling of its appeal is that childhood memories led a remarkable number of translators to work on a poem that they, too, had accepted in youthful innocence as faithful to its tribal origins. In "The Universal Hiawatha," Joe Lockard describes how translations internationalized the poem and helped shape popular literary conceptions of the American "Indian" abroad. The novelist and Nobel laureate Ivan Bunin published his Russian translation in the 1890s. "I was working with ardent love for a book that was dear to me since childhood, and with great conscientiousness," he recalled, "as this was a small homage of my gratitude to a great poet who gave me much pure and lofty joy." The poet, translator, and physician Saul Tschernichowsky remembered his introduction through a Russian translation: "I was a child when I first read *Hiawatha*. . . . My soul was bound to that song and my love was faithful until I was able to read it in the original. Who can fathom my feelings as I first read it in its entirety! . . . I translated several passages aloud to the sound of seagulls screaming." Legend has it that Tschernichowsky learned English so he could read the poem in its "original" language, then convert it into Hebrew, a task he completed in 1913 as his first major translated work.

Ironies of tangled fictions become more glaring with the poem's translation from English back into "Chippewa" by a Canadian Pacific Railroad official for an outdoor opera casting Native players. The railroad published the libretto *Hiawatha, or Nanabozho: An Ojibway Indian Play* as a lakeside tourist attraction in 1901, even inviting Longfellow's daughters to be received as honorary tribal members. "Especially it is a marked homage from American Indians [for] a white person to be so received," related one newspaper, "and yet we may take it that these surviving redmen expressed a deep and sincere national feeling in electing the poet's daughters as daughters of their tribes. They have, furthermore, done wisely as well as kindly, for the song of 'Hiawatha' is a beautiful memorial and an eloquent plea for their race and their history."

During my island stay, I found a copy of the poem published in 1992 by the British Everyman Library at Chequamegon Books, a local bookseller on the nearby mainland. In the volume's introduction, emeritus Harvard professor Daniel Aaron refers to Schoolcraft as the "indefatigable pioneer ethnologist" who introduced Longfellow (also a Harvard professor) to the "mysteries of the Indian spirit world." Aaron adds, "No dripping scalps or scenes of torture or scatological humour stain the pages of *Hiawatha*" and memorable passages "retain a faint aroma of their Indian sources, purged, to be sure, of primitive terror."

Gerald Vizenor has described Manabozho, or Nanabozho, as the "shadow name" of the sacred Anishinaabe woodland trickster, "an ironic creator and, in the same instance, the contradiction of creation." Narratives of the "teases" of creation are in Vizenor's words "suspensive, an ironic survivance" for "trickster metaphors are contradiction not representation of culture." The works of Schoolcraft and Longfellow posed as extant remains of tribal narratives. Neither man could understand Earth itself as a trickster creation. Instead they wrote false obituaries. And as a child I honored their elegies rather than the continuing presence of vital, fluid cultures.

· · ·

Attitudes and actions of government officials looking west in the early nineteenth century crafted the frame within which Henry Schoolcraft's work and writings could flourish. A letter from a former president to the head of the War Department's new Office of Indian Affairs outlined key concerns: "Next to the case of the black race within our bosom," James Madison observed to Thomas L. McKenney early in 1826, "that of the red on our borders, is the problem most baffling to the policy of our Country."

Almost eight years earlier, President James Monroe announced in his second annual message to Congress a planned military defense network along what the United States then claimed as its remote northern and northwestern frontiers. John C. Calhoun, Monroe's secretary of war, had designed the plan to end the tugs of war and politics with Britain over control of territory and the fur trade. This only three years after the War of 1812 had ended. Monroe also identified another goal in his message: "It can hardly be presumed while such posts are maintained in the rear of the Indian tribes that they will venture to attack our peaceable inhabitants. A strong hope is entertained that this measure will likewise be productive of much good to the tribes themselves, especially in promoting the great object of their civilization."

Several reconnaissance expeditions would attempt to forward both goals of defense and civilization. As governor of the Michigan Territory, Lewis Cass proposed an "exploratory tour" in the fall of 1819 through a domain that also included what are now Wisconsin and part of Minnesota. He had both political and "scientific" goals in mind. By scouting Lake Superior's southern shore and the upper reaches of the Mississippi River, the group could determine if a water "communication" linked lake and river. Cass also wanted to assess the allegiances of Anishinaabe, Dakota, and other Native peoples to the United States and its fur trade. How might they respond to ceding land or to sharing what remained with remnants of nations relocated from the east? Secretary Calhoun added Henry Schoolcraft to the expedition as mineralogist-geologist, hoping to learn the truth of long-rumored copper deposits along the lake's southern shore.

The explorers crossed more than four thousand miles by tour's end in September 1820. The reports Schoolcraft submitted to Calhoun and Congress, and an article in the *American Journal of Science,* were among the first American accounts of the Superior region's mineral riches. Noting arable soil and potential freshwater fisheries as well, all involved reached the "scientific" conclusion that the land was suitable for rapid expansion. The next step was to claim it.

Just months after receiving Madison's letter in 1826, Thomas McKenney would accompany Governor Cass and "Indian agent" Schoolcraft to the western edge of Lake Superior where they'd negotiate a treaty. The Council of Fond du Lac would be the first direct treating negotiation between the Anishinaabe around Madeline Island and the United States government. "This copper does you no good," Cass argued to tribal leaders, "and it would be useful to us to make into kettles, buttons, bells, and a great many other things." McKenney offered these words: "Friends and Brothers,—We will have good things to tell your great father who lives towards the rising sun. We will tell him his Chippeway children are men, and great men; that during this Council they behaved well; that they listened like good children to his counsel." Signed or marked on August 5, 1826, this treaty would be one of many to erode Indigenous rights to homeland. Article 3 got to the point: "The Chippewa tribe grant to the Government of the United States the right to search for, and carry away, any metals or minerals from any part of their country."

Wary of traveling "six hundred miles beyond the limits of civilization," McKenney felt lucky to have a guide, for "few men have so intimate a knowledge of Indian character as Governor Cass." Agencies under the governor's authority in the Michigan Territory dispossessed tribal peoples of millions of acres by stepwise treaty cessions. Later, as Andrew Jackson's secretary of war, Lewis Cass implemented forcible removals of Choctaw, Creek, Cherokee, and other southeastern tribal peoples across the Mississippi River. He wrote in the *North American Review* in 1830 that Americans cannot regret "the progress of civilization and improvement, the triumph of industry and art, by which these regions have been reclaimed, and over which freedom, religion, and science are extending their sway." Perhaps this progress, he acknowledged, could have been made with less harsh measures if "the aboriginal population had accommodated themselves to the inevitable change of their condition. . . . But such a wish is vain. A barbarous people, depending for subsistence upon the scanty and precarious supplies furnished by the chase, cannot live in contact with a civilized community." McKenney believed civilization's triumph required proper education by assimilation. Intergenerational ties to culture and tribal identity had to be severed, Native languages and traditions rejected. Both men have been called early architects of federal "Indian" policy.

More treaties would be made by U.S. commissioners with the Anishinaabe. Negotiations in 1837 ceded woodlands well south of Lake Superior that were soon felled by axes. Bands by the lake took notice. "I have nothing to say about the treaty, good or bad, because the country was not mine; but when it comes my turn I shall know how to act," responded Chief Buffalo of the La Pointe band on Madeline Island. "When it comes my turn to sell my land, I do not think I shall give it up as they did." His turn would come in five years when, still lured by copper, the War Department sought control of the lake's southern shore. The 1842 Treaty of La Pointe, in what the United States then claimed as the Territory of Wisconsin, explicitly ordered that "Indians residing on the Mineral district, shall be subject to removal therefrom at the pleasure of the President of the United States." The tactics used by the treaty commissioner were a bit less than honest. Robert Stuart told those gathered at La Pointe that the "Great Father" in Washington "knows that you are poor, that your lands are not good, and that you have very little game left, to feed and clothe your women & children—He therefore pities your condition, and has sent me to see what can be done to benefit you." Stuart then pressed. He assured tribal leaders that they wouldn't have to leave their homeland for many years to come, disregarding Chief Buffalo and others who opposed the terms. But the Office of Indian Affairs would try to relocate them as copper boomed. In late 1850 one attempt at removal to Sandy Lake, Minnesota, ended in the deaths of perhaps four hundred by disease, exposure, and hunger. Bands then tried to resist, even sending delegations to Washington, D.C.

But in 1854 Wisconsin had been a state for six years. A few thousand Anishinaabe gathered again on Madeline Island at La Pointe that September to finalize the treaty ceding land on Lake Superior's shore and establishing reserved tracts in Wisconsin, Michigan, and Minnesota. The first signatories were from the La Pointe Band, the first to sign Ke-che-waish-ke, or the Buffalo, first chief. La Pointe bands relocated to permanent reservations on the nearby mainland within their territory, at Bad River and Red Cliff. Gerald Vizenor's ancestors, among the crane families, finally were removed to the White Earth Reservation in Minnesota in 1868.

Apostle Islands National Lakeshore embraces most of the archipelago and part of the mainland Bayfield Peninsula. It lies within territory ceded by treaty and partly within the reservations of the Red Cliff Band of Lake Superior Chippewa Indians and the Bad River Band of the Lake Superior Tribe of Chippewa Indians. (In 2012 the Red Cliff Band set aside eighty-nine acres of boreal forest and shoreline as Frog Bay Tribal National Park, the first such reserve of its kind.) Anishinaabe people still negotiate for the right to use ceded land on the lakeshore in accordance with the 1842 and 1854 treaties. Mining continues to threaten treaty rights elsewhere.

· · ·

For author Louise Erdrich, the painted islands west of Lake Superior in Lake of the Woods are book-islands to be read. Her grandfather was the last person in her family to speak Anishinaabemowin with any fluency. So she tried to acquire what she had not been taught: an intimate engagement with "the spirit of the words" and thus with the land itself. She learned, for instance, that the word for stone—*asin*—is animate. "After all," she writes, "the preexistence of the world according to Ojibwe religion consisted of a conversation between stones." For geologists who by and large conduct their work steeped in the traditions of Western science, Lake Superior's book-islands have told other stories.

One I learned is that the ancestral frameworks and most aged rocks of the world's continents lie within their exposed nuclei, the Precambrian shields. As remnants of an inconceivably distant past, shields chronicle many evolutions: the early growth of continents, origins of life, and an atmosphere gradually becoming habitable. The southernmost outcrops of North America's core, the Canadian Shield, rim Lake Superior.

The Midcontinent Rift also lies exposed here. I learned that it, too, is another piece of North America's ancient architecture, and geoscientists lean toward superlatives in describing a feature most people have never heard of. They say this rift is among the largest outpourings of lava in the world. It's one of the longest ancient rifts on any continent, rivaling that in east Africa where our species emerged. The Midcontinent Rift is also among the finest examples of a continent's initial splitting apart that then "aborted," or stopped cold. Had the crack continued to open, a new sea might have flooded the void. But, for whatever reason, it ceased, an oceanic zipper just partly undone. Rift rocks around Lake Superior form the visible part of the apex of a huge almost bell-shaped band following the lake's arced shape. Geophysicists have remotely detected the band's limbs descending southward beneath a blanket of still ancient strata laid down by long-vanished inland seas across the Midwest. One limb points toward Kansas, the other beneath Michigan.

I've tried to imagine a billion years of rift highlands and flood basalts weathering and eroding. Then the Pleistocene ice ages nearly having the last word as the restless nose of the great Laurentide ice sheet pulsed forth and back until its final melting retreat northward across Canada less than ten thousand years ago. Loose earth debris that ice had scoured up and dragged across the shield now mantles the rift sandstone, bedrock of the Apostle Islands and nearby mainland. Bluffs cut into this glacial drift release cobbles to fronting beaches with each storm. These rocks are animate indeed.

Watching days end from my friend's beach, I soon realized that "scientific" research of the shield and rift began here because of what the bedrock contained. I saw, too, that choices I had made in studies and work were somehow implicated in this pursuit of mineral wealth. Men from Britain, France, and a fledgling United States "discovered" then deliberately sought copper and iron in the nineteenth century's first decades. For some like Lieutenant Henry Wolsey Bayfield, who made the first accurate chart of Lake Superior for the British Royal Navy in the 1820s, host rocks held clues to a most distant past. To him the "objects of Geology" were "to seek among the ruins of strata for the only records of those awful events which have swept whole orders of organized beings from existence. These are only to be obtained by the accumulation of facts." By the 1880s geologists well versed in the state of the science had accumulated many "facts" by tramping and mapping the lake's mainland and islands. They described faults suggestive of Precambrian rifting. They recognized the terrain's underlying structure as a bowl-shaped pile of thousands of stratified feet of once molten magma capped by sandstone—which they named "Keweenawan." Even Henry Schoolcraft had observed what he called the "Old Red Sandstone of Lake Superior" overlying "traprock" (basalt) and granite while on Governor Cass's exploratory tour in 1820. And, more than a century ago, Charles R. Van Hise and Charles K. Leith admitted the impetus of research in *The Geology of the Lake Superior Region*, their seven-hundred-page monograph for the U.S. Geological Survey: "The great development of the mineral industry in this region has afforded the geologist unusual opportunity for study, as it has not only made the region more accessible but has justified larger expenditures for geologic study than would otherwise have been made."

Paths toward understanding the history and architecture of this landscape didn't begin in a contextual vacuum, and published science's specialized passive voice can frustrate a reader interested in agency. I've come up short, in text after text, searching through "facts" underpinning current scientific models of the region's most ancient past and of the origins of rich metal ores. Yet on this southern shore of Lake Superior I saw that one path accompanied (driving and benefiting from) a state-sponsored search for minerals and the confinement of Anishinaabe people on reservations. By 1890, less than half a century after the removals, the ceded lands led the world in copper mined.

Tumultuous histories, human and geological, formed this landscape in which I am implicated. And they continue. The current move to mine iron in the nearby Penokee Range, watershed of the Bad River Band of the Lake Superior Tribe of Chippewa Indians, threatens not only tribal sovereignty and treaty rights but also the wild rice sloughs along the lakeshore that ancestors harvested for generations.

• • •

On clouded days lake and sky share the same cast, no line marking one from the other. Once autumn opened the country, limits to distance fell away with birch and aspen leaves.

Time and space merged—I was the adult who felt again that searching child of seven and ten.

Each evening on the island beach, I could touch more than a hundred stones lying within arm's reach. Each cobble a relic of a remote past *and* a piece of and in this present. These fragments of placed-memory could trace, to the geologist's eye, a continent's coming of age as it shifted and rifted in a tectonic-plated world. They also pointed north toward ghosts of ice sheets grinding across the shield.

The events of one's life take place, too. Our lives take place. In movements large and small. Of the Anishinaabe becoming a people indigenous to the particularities of these woodlands and lakes. Of newcomers searching for minerals, settling the old Michigan and Wisconsin territories, displacing those so very long-placed. My time here measuring the motions of seasons and days. The arrival of what Roger Tory Peterson called "confusing fall warblers" to announce September. The shifting of shoreline stones with each wave swash.

Taking place has other dimensions, too. Of choices and practices aimed at possessing and controlling both territory and ideas of it. The pursuit of knowledge, of "scientific" research, wasn't innocent here as Indigenous traditions and people, as the land itself, were objectified and commodified, mined and collected. Any attempt to disentangle the search for copper or iron (or nickel or gold) from those first scientific studies, from treatied dispossessings, or from early American ethnography is a fool's errand.

In their mappings and renamings, agents from Europe and Euro-America claimed already inhabited and named terrain. Henry Rowe Schoolcraft "discovered" a river source that was well known. *The Song of Hiawatha*—marker of an authentic "indigenous" American literature—appeared within a year of the treaty dispossessing the people whom the poem supposedly honored. Schoolcraft, Lewis Cass, and others became experts by *re*-defining, *re*-positioning, *re*-presenting, and thus obscuring animate lives within this land to those looking from without. Gerald Vizenor has called their discoveries "the very cause of absence not the presence of natives." Yet the lives and traditions of these tribal people remained an active evolving presence. Vizenor's "survivance" is important here. Meaning more than survival, more than endurance or mere response, stories of survivance embrace shadow, tease, creation, motion, and coherence. They resist fixed categories or deadening stereotypes. "The shadows of tribal names and stories are the ventures of landscapes, even in the distance of translation," he writes. "Tribal imagination, experience, and remembrance, are the real landscapes in the literature of this nation; discoveries and dominance are silence."

At Lake Superior's shore I gazed at a self-reflection of old lessons and older assumptions. I saw yet again how long absences also lay formative within me. At seven I felt honored to know and trust a true Indian story in *The Song of Hiawatha*. My deep interest in America's past and its places was propelled by fifth-grade lessons that romanticized Henry Schoolcraft's exploits as heroic. Inventions clothed me. Yet I couldn't easily see what wasn't my own as not being my own. The emotional dearness of certain memories remains formative. A dearness that has kept them vital and immediate, as if I could reach that little girl drawing the wigwam of Nokomis in the sky.

Perhaps on Madeline Island I began to catch up with the past, but not in Constance Fenimore Woolson's sense. Her novel *Anne*, a tale of a Great Lakes island in the 1880s, found me from the shelves of Chequamegon Books. It opened at this passage: "Unless, indeed, the past should come back—a possibility which did not seem so unlikely on the island as it does elsewhere, since the people were plainly retrograding, and who knows but that they might some time even catch up with the past?" Catching up with the past need not mean retrograding or living in it. At least I hope not. Dissecting learned stories might yield some retrievable fragments of context and relationship, and reveal the vector of storying's power—its direction, its magnitude, and its agency.

I cannot be a complete stranger to the past or to a place such as this. These woodlands and I are partly effaced palimpsests. Altered in the passage of time, yes, but still retaining traces of earlier forms and origins. Here, Gerald Vizenor's lessons come home to me. To understand the storying of any place, I must also understand the storying of myself. I must follow traces beneath familiar surfaces to where ancestral structures lie.

With these thoughts I turned to my father's box.

WHAT'S IN A NAME

Give me a story, and I'll give you one in return.

Anyone passing our yard might think the solitary child played with an imaginary friend. She'd twirl in place, arms outstretched, eyes closed. Each turn bringing a new word spoken with care. *Sequoia. Shenandoah. Cheyenne. Susquehanna. Mojave. Yosemite. Wyoming.* The words were names that rolled off her tongue. She'd stop, then spin the other way. *Potomac. Chesapeake. Narragansett. Appomattox.*

Once given breath, the names incanted spells, the turns crossing all distance between place and child. These weren't turns of fancy but a melding of sound and Earth *in* her—in my—mind's eye and ear, much as evening shadows overtook the house edge, then approached and included me. Soundings touched contours of mysterious stories that could be plumbed if asked. *Give me a story. I'll give you one in return.*

"Names are magic. One word can pour such a flood through the soul." Had I at the age of six understood Walt Whitman's words, I would have counted him friend. Word-moments could blaze with an intensity that seemed to concentrate all life. I placed myself by the compass of places sung aloud. That I hadn't yet set foot in most mattered little. There were other ways to travel to them.

Once the alphabet was no longer a stranger, books joined road maps as primers. *Green Eggs and Ham* shared a shelf with folded offerings from Flying A and Esso, Chevron and the Automobile Club of Southern California. My father's cast-offs became templates for storied wanderings. The painted cover of one map opened the scene of a story that would always end the same bright way: The gas station attendant sports a smile and pressed white uniform as he greets a family in a station wagon. Clouds glow above a golden evening sun. The two-lane highway switch-backs toward a mountain crest on the western horizon. The story continues: The attendant welcomes me and my parents. He fills our tank, checks our tires, oil, and plugs. Then he cleans our windows and tells us about the road ahead. The smile never wanes. With thank-yous exchanged Daddy pulls back onto the highway. We'll cross the pass on our way home to 1253 Redondo Boulevard, Los Angeles, California.

This is happy motoring.

The names scattered across that map's paper landscape would have taken flight if not for the roads and highways stitching them down. Thick and thin, solid and dashed, red and blue, they linked El Monte to the San Gabriel Mountains, Death Valley to Owens Valley, Kings Canyon to Tulare, Big Sur to Monterey Bay. Geography triangulated to Redondo Boulevard. To read a map meant I could reach any place on it. "You were born on the highway," my mother would joke. It seemed a simple statement of fact. Even Nat King Cole sang to me: *wild and windblown, that's how you've grown, who can cling to a ramblin' rose.*

ERWIN RAISZ'S LARGE landforms map of the continental United States lies unrolled on the floor as these memories surface. Drawn by the precise hand of a master cartographer-artist, the map was last revised years before my birth. It shows no highways or other overlays of commercial road maps, save state boundaries, cities, and some towns. Raisz's pen strokes outline his sense of the land's texture. His lines are the paths of sinuous rivers, the edges of plateaus, the summits of mountain ranges. Most names place this geography.

Creased, taped, and retaped, this map has joined me on every cross-country trip I've taken, overland or by air, since that day in college when Professor Judson handed out copies to his geomorphology class. *Read me*, it called then. It still does. So I do, and in locating where I sit this moment, where I was one, ten, and twenty years ago, memories orient me once again. From the Pacific coast over the Sierra Nevada, through the canyon and plateau country, over the Rocky Mountains and across the Great Plains to the Appalachians and Atlantic coast.

Names on the paper landscape call, too. Map details blur until I dab my eyes.

• • •

Once the continent wore no names, having no need for them. The languages of water, ice, and wind prevailed. Yet one can say *Oklahoma* or *Yellowstone* or *badlands* without thinking—so embedded are they in American vocabulary. It may be a commonplace to consider place-names or toponyms as givens, distinguishing one piece of terrain from another. To think this, though, is to see a reflecting surface and not what lies beneath.

My search for origins began years ago with George Rippey Stewart, a man who by his own admission was "born with a love of names." A professor of English at the University of California at Berkeley for decades in the last century, Stewart scaled walls between literary genres and academic fields. His writings include a history of the Donner Party and novels like the best-selling *Storm*, which featured a Pacific cyclone he called Maria.

Of his nearly thirty books, Stewart's own favorite was *Names on the Land*, a "historical account of place-naming in the United States" that appeared at the end of the Second World War. "Thus the names lay thickly over the land," Stewart wrote in the opening pages, "and the Americans spoke them, great and little, easily and carelessly—Virginia, Susquehanna, Rio Grande, Deadman Creek, Sugarloaf Hill, Detroit, Wall Street—not thinking how they had come to be. Yet the names had grown out of the life, and the life-blood, of all those who had gone before." *Names on the Land* tells stories of patterns and motives. It moved many writers of American places. Wallace Stegner, for one, acknowledged his debt to Stewart for clarifying "our history, or tradition, the story of our five-hundred-year love/hate struggle with the North American continent," which "is there in the names we have put on the land." Stegner thought Stewart's books "teach us who we are, and how we got to be who we are." Many agree. *The New York Review of Books* reissued *Names on the Land* in its classics series in 2008. The introduction to this edition calls it a "masterpiece of American writing and American history" produced by an "informed imagination that animates the past and instills . . . the spark and majesty of life."

The narrative sweep and folkloric detail moved me, too. So did disappointment—for not "all those who had gone before," or who came later, had voice in this extraordinary volume. The toponyms that most concerned Stewart either originated with voyagers and colonists from Europe and their heirs, or filtered through them from Indigenous tongues, sometimes so much the worse for wear that "the names became more European than Indian." And "when tribes and languages had vanished," he noted, "some of those old names, reshaped, lived still in the speech of those who followed."

Traveling at a reasonable clip across the page, I tripped and fell here. *When tribes and languages had vanished. Vanish* is a deceptive word. It slips easily off the tongue, the soft *sh* a finger to lips quieting a history far from simple, neat, or finished. The earliest encountered tribal peoples along North America's Atlantic Seaboard whose communities were disrupted longest—like the Wampanoag or Powhatan—didn't simply vanish. Fragmented, dispossessed of land, dislocated, perhaps ravaged by disease and violence, tribal peoples endured. Members reorganized or joined other groups. They migrated or they stayed in smaller communities. They continued to speak.

Names on the Land carries a sympathetic tone regarding Native peoples, but it is the stories of "those who followed" from Europe that form its core. What troubles me is how some readers embrace these namings as America's history, "our" heritage, without asking if there might be other narratives, too. Stewart considers "the naming that was before history" in his first chapter, but not so much the importance of place-making in defining Indigenous traditions and identities in a storied land over time. And what of names and practices left by those from Africa and Asia who'd come to this continent? Perhaps readers assume they left no mark.

. . .

I was born in the homeland of the Ohlone, which Spain claimed as part of Alta California. My parents and I lived at first in a city by a bay named for Saint Francis of Assisi. We then moved south to another city, grown around a river now confined within a concrete channel. That settlement was called El Pueblo de la Reina de los Angeles de la Porciúncula. One of the mountains in the range west of it came to be known as "Niggerhead." Then we crossed the continent to what had been part of the Piscataway chiefdom and claimed by Great Britain. We settled in a capital city named to honor the first president of the new American republic. Few of the official names of these places, east or west, arose from the land itself.

I now live in New England, a half hour's drive from New Hampshire. On road trips south, I pass through New York and New Jersey. There are other "new" places. New Londons and New Bostons. New Brunswick and Nova Scotia. Names appear again and again. Cambridge, Bristol, Portsmouth, Newport, Plymouth, more— each having found at least two homes in the British colonies.

In the Chesapeake Bay area that became my paternal ancestors' home, names paid homage to monarchs whose patronage voyagers either enjoyed or sought. Virginia for a virgin queen Elizabeth. Jamestown and James, settlement and river, remembering a king. Terra Mariae (Maryland) acknowledging another queen, Henrietta Maria, wife to Charles, son of James. Then there are the Syracuses, Troys, Athenses, Romes, Alexandrias, and Philadelphias scattered across American maps to recall an older Old World. Other names spread westward, too, with Anglo-American settlers after the Revolution. They left the land, as H. L. Mencken put it, "bespattered with *Washingtons, Lafayettes, Jeffersons* and *Jacksons*." Columbuses, Columbias, Madisons, and, later, Lincolns joined them.

Colonial tugs of war left remnants in name-clusters born of other languages. I hear Dutch echoes on every trip by New York City: Haarlem or Haerlem, Jonkheer's (Yonkers), de Bouwerij (the Bowery). Streets named Breede Wegh (Broadway) and De Waal (Wall). Nassau, Flushing, Staten, the Bronx. To the north, Poughkeepsie and Peekskill; across the Hudson River, Hopoakan and Hackensack. Breukelen's "broken land" a nod to Long Island's glacial debris.

I also hear lasting marks of Spain: California, Florida, Nueva México. Santa Fe, San Francisco, Trinidad, Santa Cruz, Los Angeles. Oasis meadows of Las Vegas. Sierra Nevada, the snowy range. Rio Grande del Norte, great river of the north. Colorado, mud-red river. *Cañon, mesa, arroyo, playa*—terms for dryland features that English didn't know.

"FOR NAME, THOUGH it seem but a superficial and outward matter," wrote Francis Bacon, "yet it carrieth much impression and enchantment." Names encode meaning and memory. I can understand the impulse to place the linguistic familiar about oneself. In stapling down small created certainties, an overlain geography of home could then orient and transform a vast unknown into a knowable new chance. Naming and mapping would work as twin projects in the courses of empire, as semantic (re)defining fit a design that made sense to the ambitions of those men from Europe who made landfall after landfall.

Their linguistic claiming overprinted and appropriated older names, other views already there. Colonial maps and place-names reorganized space on a slate made blank—by drawing borders, by coding what (and whom) lay inside or out, by erasing. Columbus couldn't hear Taíno speech, or at least he rationalized that they had no language by which to embrace the Holy Faith. He shipped captives back to Spain "in order that they might learn to speak." The admiral then named and named and named, for God and Spain, islands, waterways, and coasts known by other terms.

The project of illuminating terra incognita's darkness made certain ways of inhabiting and relating to this place called "America" natural. It made particular points of view normal. In their place-making these newcomers not only set out to possess territory on the ground. They also lay claim to territory of the mind and memory, to the future and the past.

The people who were already there—Taíno, Powhatan, Wampanoag, and countless others—who now were discovered but still not seen, could and did look back.

Here lies a paradox. To become oriented, to find their way and fill their maps, venturers from Europe needed Native peoples' knowledge of the land. Maps and names would then obscure that knowledge from its context, as Indigenous people themselves were removed from the land.

A pot spilled. Perceptions and names spread inland from the Atlantic Seaboard, up from Mexico and the Caribbean, covering older names and ideas. Names come into view but sink from sight. Names metamorphose.

I look for those rooted in Native America. I look, too, for visions originating with newcomers from continents other than Europe. What I seek, of course, are linguistic seeds of my own presence.

NATIVE PLACE-NAMES, OR the names of tribal people living in those places, began to appear on sixteenth- and seventeenth-century European maps inland of the Atlantic coast. It might be better to say that explorers and colonists transcribed into familiar symbols what they heard. Indigenous sounds twisted on European, then Anglo-American tongues. Words and phrases were often reshaped with little sense of original context or use. Maps and journals then carried forward clipped words, simplified renderings, and transliterated sounds. Mutating steps could result in an English version of a French interpretation of an Indigenous word that ended up as Wisconsin. In misreading hand-drawn sketches, map-makers and engravers in Europe created more errors. One changed letter, once formalized in print, could make a name of great meaning become meaningless.

More than half of the United States' names originated, in some form, from Indigenous languages. Some began as records of tribal peoples encountered, either what they called themselves or what others called them. Dakota, Illini, Kansa, Ute. Some state names refer to specific elements of the landscape. Massachusett, to the Wampanoag, means "place of the foothill," but Puritan settlers used it for a bay and their colony. Kwinitekw, the long tidal river, became Connecticut. And there is the convoluted origin of the name Wisconsin. According to George Stewart, the French voyageurs Jolliet and Marquette heard and recorded Mesconsing (or Mescousing) in 1673 for a river flowing west to the continental interior. But Mesconsing became Ouisconsing or Ouisconsink on later maps, finally Wisconsin in English.

Native words for aspects of waterways, or of names of people living by them, also persist, even if in altered forms. Potomac. Rappahannock. Susquehanna. Merrimac. Penobscot. Connecticut. Ohio. Wabash. Missouri. Mississippi. Chesapeake. All but one of the Great Lakes. Stewart described a shallow, braided river crossing the plains that was called Ni-bthaska in one Native language, *ni* for "river" and *bthaska* for its spreading flatness. Frenchmen in the 1700s translated this name to Rivière Plate, but spelled it Platte. These waters became the lifeline of the Oregon Trail—and from Ni-bthaska, Stewart noted, came the name of one state through which the river flows.

Place-names that might or might not have been bestowed by Indigenous people for those places shimmer like mirages. I live in Massachusetts. I've swum in the Connecticut River. I've spent long hours by the Potomac and Susquehanna Rivers, by Chesapeake Bay. I've waded into the Platte, the Arkansas, the Missouri. I've crossed the Mississippi's headwaters on stepping-stones. And I've explored mountains. Adirondack. Taconic. Ouachita. Pocono. Wasatch. Absaroka. Uinta. Appalachian.

The long range stretching from Alabama to Newfoundland is ancient, its contours the worn roots of peaks thought once as grand as the Alps. For Stewart its name began with a 1528 search for gold in Florida. As chronicled by Álvar Núñez Cabeza de Vaca, the ill-fated Narváez expedition found no gold but encountered Native people and a village called Apalchen, Apalachen, or Apalache. This name would appear in various spellings on Spanish, French, and other maps as a marker for the mysterious interior. Even Mercator's 1569 map of the world placed Apalchen near a large river flowing between the two southern prongs of a long chain of mountains paralleling the east coast. Travelers from Europe and Anglo-American settlers would use various names up and down the chain, but by the late 1700s Allegheny (or Alleghany) and Appalachian vied for the entire length. After Arnold Guyot published "On the Appalachian Mountain System," his study of the range's elevations and structure, in 1861, that name's usage slowly began to spread. It could have gone the other way: Guyot's map, prepared before he finished the report, used Alleghany.

In my mind, though, Oregon and Wyoming offer the most telling examples of how far out of linguistic and geographic context American place-naming could reach.

The Oregon story George Stewart favored began with a coincidence of mistakes on a 1715 map, an old legend that hadn't yet died, and liberties taken by explorer-promoters who claimed and advertised far more than they knew. First, a map-engraver misspelled the Ouisconsink River (already a mutated word) as "Ouaricon-sint," placing the hyphen and last four letters beneath the rest of the name. The crowded map showed the Ouaricon flowing west from the Great Lakes region. A later, more fanciful map applied the name to the fabled River to the West, which legend had flowing from the midcontinent through the Rocky Mountains to the Pacific Ocean. Ouaricon passed into Ouragon, Ourigan, and finally to the name now used.

Wyoming also began as an eastern Indigenous term that migrated west. The name of a valley in northeastern Pennsylvania, it might be a corrupted version of a Lenape word for "at the big flats" or "great meadows." It became wildly popular among Anglo-Americans after an 1809 poem by Thomas Campbell, "Gertrude of Wyoming," memorialized three hundred settlers killed by British loyalists and Iroquois allies in 1778. Ten Wyoming post offices sprang up between Rhode Island and Nebraska within six decades. The name was also proposed for a new territory organizing north of Colorado after the Civil War. Debates in both the U.S. House of Representatives and Senate would prove the longest on the floor of Congress over land naming. Against the use of Wyoming was the obvious incongruity between name and place. Tribal names from the area were then considered. Cheyenne received the most attention until one senator suggested it sounded too close to the French word for a female dog, *chienne*. We know the end of the story. The reasons that won the day? Euphony and poetic association, or as Wisconsin senator James Doolittle offered, "Because it is a beautiful name." So it is, one of my childhood favorites to sing aloud. Wyoming Territory was established on July 25, 1868.

THE USE OF Native or native-sounding words as place-names grew ever more popular among Anglo-Americans through the nineteenth century. Washington Irving so favored them that he proposed the country be called Appalachia or, better still, Alleghania.

Walt Whitman, too, praised Indigenous names that "roll[ed] with venison richness upon the palate." He'd set out in the 1850s to celebrate the language of the United States in *An American Primer*. "All the greatness of any land, at any time, lies folded in its names," Whitman wrote. "Words follow character,—nativity, independence, individuality," elements that he believed set the United States and Americans apart. Being "of the national blood," Indigenous words that gave a "taste of identity and locality" contributed to this unique American character. "I was asking for something

savage and luxuriant," he expanded, "and behold, here are the aboriginal names. . . . They are honest words,—they give the true
length, breadth, depth. They all fit. Mississippi!—the word winds
with chutes—it rolls a stream three thousand miles long. Ohio,
Connecticut, Ottawa, Monongahela, all fit."

Whitman never finished *An American Primer*. His companion
and literary executor finally shepherded it into print in *The Atlantic
Monthly* in 1904, half a century after its bulk had been penned,
twelve years after the poet's death. But as Whitman had hoped,
the primer went on to influence another generation of writers.
H. L. Mencken acknowledged and matched Whitman's fervor in
The American Language, his landmark study of the development
of American English. He, too, was taken by "native" words. "Such
names as Tallahassee, Susquehanna, Mississippi, Allegheny, Chi-
cago, Kennebec, Patuxent and Kalamazoo give a barbaric brilliancy
to the American map," Mencken wrote in the 1921 edition. "Only
the map of Australia can match it."

Both men had researched toponyms in the official lists of post
offices. Mencken also drew from the reports of the U.S. Board
on Geographic Names, whose mandate was to steer the country
toward standardized place-name usage. Accented letters, names
with multiple words, names with articles, suffixes, and apostrophes
all fell prey as the board anglicized and simplified terms from many
languages for the sake of "official" uniformity. La Cygne, in Kansas,
became Lacygne. Portage des Flacons lost to Bottle Portage. El
Dorado squeezed into Eldorado, De Laux to Dlo. "In its laudable
effort to simplify American nomenclature," Mencken lamented
that the board had "played ducks and drakes with some of the most
picturesque names on the national map."

I stop, again, to scan the hand-drawn map by Erwin Raisz. The
American landscape is palimpsest. Layers upon layers of names
and meanings lie beneath the official surface. What came *before*

colonial maps and names was vast and long. On the eve of contact the breath-taking diversity of Native languages exceeded that of Europe—at least several hundred distinct languages were spoken north of Mexico, perhaps thousands in the Western Hemisphere.

Imagine the names. Imagine their origins.

WHILE MANY INDIGENOUS languages ceased to be spoken over five eroding and assimilating centuries, hundreds survive in the Americas, even with the looming threat of silence as fluent speakers age and die. Some tribal groups, like the Wampanoag Nation, work to reclaim as a primary means of expression what had been nearly lost.

The land may be the "matrix" of linguistic meaning for oral cultures. Leslie Marmon Silko has described how "the continuity and accuracy of oral narratives are reinforced by the landscape" for Laguna Pueblo people. In *Wisdom Sits in Places: Landscape and Language among the Western Apache*, Keith Basso notes that "place-names are arguably among the most highly charged and richly evocative of all linguistic symbols." A linguistic anthropologist, Basso had cowboyed with and worked among the Western Apache (Ndee) for years when an elder asked for help in making Apache maps of their land near the Salt River in eastern Arizona. Basso came to understand the sacred, indivisible nature of place and words for these people. Theirs is a language that situates ancestral knowledge (*nohwizá'yé bi kigoyá'íí*) and traditional narratives, mind and heart, time and space in the lives of a person and a people. The Ndee word *ni'* means both land and mind, calling on the inseparability of place and thought. In *ni'*, Earth and thinking converge: "Wisdom sits in places."

Basso learned that the evocative power of place-names is "most forcefully displayed when a name is used to substitute for the narrative it anchors, 'standing up alone' (*'o'áá*), as Apaches say, to symbolize the narrative as well as the knowledge it contains." A place, its name, and other ancestral narratives emergent there cannot be separated. The land watches over and "stalks" the people as a cultural mnemonic of origins, of "purposive" behavior. What's crucial is to "think and act 'with' [landscapes] as well as about and upon them, and to weave them with spoken words into the very foundations of social life." As one example of "*sensing* of place," Basso recalls an incident while stringing barbed wire with two Apache cowboys. He noticed one man reciting a long list of place-names in between spurts of tobacco juice. Asked why, the man responded that he "talked names" all the time. "I ride that way in my mind."

N. Scott Momaday has referred to woven experiences of imagination, language, and place—and the relationships born of them—as "reciprocal appropriation." To invest oneself in the land while incorporating the land into one's "own most fundamental experience." Place-making is both a way of "*doing* human history," Basso offers, as well as "a way of constructing social traditions and, in the process, personal and social identities. We *are*, in a sense, the place-worlds we imagine."

· · ·

66 In contrast to the oppressed Indian," George Stewart concluded in *Names on the Land*, "the oppressed African left little mark upon the map. Pinder Town in South Carolina preserved the Kongo *mpinda*, 'peanut,' but white men probably did the naming after the word had become current in local speech. Doubtless many hundreds of small streams and swamps were named by Negroes, but their namings cannot be distinguished."

Left little mark upon the map. Their namings cannot be distinguished. A dismissal unlikely to be questioned by most. But as diaspora linguists like Annette Kashif have observed, languages and naming patterns from Africa crossed the Atlantic, too. Toponyms bearing their influence survive on the land and on maps, especially along the coast and tidewater rivers of the South. That these names have been overlooked beyond a few studies is, I know, part of the story.

Some place-names with at least partial roots in Africa were long thought either irresolvable mysteries or of solely Indigenous origin. Suwannee stumped William Read in his *Florida Place-Names of Indian Origin and Seminole Personal Names* (1934): "The name . . . cannot be translated with certainty, the lack of historical data rendering futile all guesses at its etymology." Suwannee always summons to mind two songs I learned in childhood. Stephen Foster's "Old Folks at Home" from 1851 is still Florida's state song. It's easy to imagine Christy's Minstrels in blackface "a-longin'" for the old plantation." Quick on this tune's heels I hear Al Jolson singing, "Swanee, how I love ya, how I love ya, my dear old Swanee!" Yet two possible African sources for the word include *nsub'wanyi* for "my house" or "my home" in Kongo or Mbundu, and the West African (Mandingo) *Suwane*, a personal name.

Suwannee also hints at twining relations among southeastern tribal peoples and Africans, ties far more tangled than stories of harbored fugitives or enslaved workers imply. From their earliest presence in Atlantic and Caribbean colonies, enslaved peoples escaped bondage to establish *maroon* camps in remote, inaccessible areas. The Great Dismal Swamp, straddling Virginia and North Carolina's low-country border, was one such refuge. Suwannee Old Town was a Seminole-African community along the Suwannee River sacked by Andrew Jackson's forces in 1818.

Though some findings have been questioned, Winifred Vass posited African roots for other American place-names. Combahee in Mississippi from *kombahu* or "sweep here" (imperative). Ulah in North Carolina from *ula*, possibly meaning "to purchase" or "buy."

Nakina, North Carolina, from *nuakina*, "to hate" or "to be cruel."
Alcolu, South Carolina, perhaps from *alakana*, meaning "to long
for, hope for, desire greatly." These are but a few. And hybrid words
admixing tongues from two or more continents may be more
common than once thought.

What disturbs me is how these names, if their origins bear out,
may be commentaries on life *in* those places. Buy. Hate. Home.
Deep longing.

There is no question, though, of linguistic agency with the many
communities that free and freed African Americans established over
two centuries. Parting Ways was settled near Plymouth, Massachusetts, by a small group who'd won their freedom fighting in the
Revolution. "Black towns" grew in number with the great exodus
north and west across the Mississippi River after the Civil War.
Liberty. Freedmantown. Freemanville. Lincolnville. Independence
Heights. Union City. Bookertee. Nicodemus. Blackdom. Some,
like those I'd visited in Oklahoma, succeeded. Others succumbed
within a generation.

A much more hurtful dimension lies in place-names that refer
to African Americans but weren't given by them. "Nigger" once fea-
tured in at least two hundred American toponyms according to the
U.S. Board on Geographic Names. "Dead Nigger Creek." "Dead
Nigger Hill." "Nigger Canyon." "Nigger Slough." "Nigger Ford."
"Nigger Lake." "Nigger Gulch." "Nigger Spring." "Nigger Head
Peak." "Nigger Head Mountain." "Niggerhead Island." "Nigger
Heel Bar." "Niggertown Marsh." "Nigger Prairie." "Nigger Joe
Ridge." "Nigger George Draw." "Nigger Bill Canyon." On and
on—in most states, from Maine to Alaska.

The NAACP and others petitioned the Board on Geographic
Names for decades to remove the word. Piecemeal changes occurred, a name revised here, another there, until the board decided
in 1963 to replace what it called the "pejorative form of Negro"

with "Negro" on federal maps and documents. But so embedded was the "pejorative form" that it continues in pockets of local speech and on some maps.

I first encountered such a place-name on a journey across the country the summer after college. Erwin Raisz's map guided me by land texture. My Honda meandered with the Colorado River on Utah Route 128 between Cisco and Moab. On an afternoon in the high nineties, finding a wading spot was a high priority. Sheer sandstone walls flanked many small tributaries of the river. The BLM trailhead sign at one of them stopped me—NEGRO BILL CANYON. Who was this Bill? Why and when was he here? Sandstone echoed my questions. Later I learned that William Granstaff or Grandstaff was a man of mixed heritage who had come in 1877 as an early pioneer and grazed cattle. "Nigger Bill" featured prominently on an old map I saw in Moab.

And a peak in the Santa Monica Mountains west of our Los Angeles home wore the name "Niggerhead." It, too, took a long linguistic journey, stopping briefly at Negrohead, then, in 2009, becoming Ballard Mountain to acknowledge this early homesteader as a man with a name.

Other slur-names remain. Or they've only recently been changed by the Board on Geographic Names. "Chink Peak" or "Chink's Peak" near Pocatello, Idaho, became Chinese Peak in 2001. "Jap Rock," in California's Solano County, was renamed Japanese Point. But many are still the official names on the land: Pickaninny Buttes, California; Wop Draw, Wyoming; Darkey Springs, Tennessee; Wetback Tank, New Mexico; Dago Gulch, Montana; Dead Injun Creek, Oregon; Sambo Creek in Pennsylvania and Alabama. On and on.

Words of enmity and ignorance that had fallen out of general favor long ago persisted as the official, formal names on the land.

Names outlive the bestowers for many reasons. I think of the vantage point, the "appearance" of overwhelming difference in the eyes and ears of beholding namers over five hundred years. Even the Linnaean system of binomial nomenclature (listing genus and species), so taken for granted as an international standard, began as part of colonial world trade that collected human beings as it collected exotic plants and animals.

Languages spoken by unknown ancestors converged toward me. But linguistic tributaries arising in Africa and Native America were cut off or diverted long ago. I speak and write in English, a language with no adjective form for *place*. My school rambles through Latin, French, and Castilian Spanish kept me mostly within Europe's realm. Sounds, gestures, rhythms from other lands, all were lost.

Yes, I am palimpsest, too, a place made over but trying to trace back.

· · ·

Years ago Barbara Ras invited me to research terms for a collection Barry Lopez was editing on a "vocabulary" grown from this land. The end product was *Home Ground: Language for an American Landscape*. My efforts played a small part in this community project, but their impact on me was immense. Old memories surfaced as I compiled a list of more than six hundred geologic, geographic, and regional folk terms for the continent's features. I began to call the words aloud.

a'a ablation hollow abra alamar alamo alkali flats . . .

badland bajada bald bally banco baraboo . . .

cajo caldera caleta cañada cañon candela cat hole catoctin . . .

A current of language and imagination, dry for so long a time, could still rise and flow, entraining me as water would a grain of sand. Language of the land still worked on me.

What lies beneath the surface of maps and names? The answers, and their layers of meaning, of course depend on one's point of view. Whether what came before 1492 is considered prelude to an American story beginning to unfold. Whether participants from places other than Europe are seen as supporting cast or props. Whether "we" and "our culture" embrace a much larger changing whole.

"All the greatness of any land, at any time, lies folded in its names," wrote Walt Whitman in his *American Primer.* "Names are the turning point of who shall be master." If history can be read in the names on the land, then the text at the surface is partial and pieced. A reader might do well to look beyond "official" maps for traces of other languages, other visions. He or she might do well to acknowledge, and mourn, the loss of innumerable names born out of textured homelands that no longer reside in living memory. We all might do well to remember that names are one measure of how one chooses to inhabit the world.

Give me a story, and I'll give you one in return.

PROPERTIES OF DESIRE

How is the past remembered and told?

Who owns memory?

Upland South Carolina that June was a thick ripening green, grown from red-rust soil on the ancient metamorphic Piedmont. Two questions caught between my breath and humid air as I walked the path from Walnut Grove's cemetery.

My friend Dorinda and I had just completed the plantation tour; we wanted to see more of the grounds. In a small clearing at the end of a footpath, marble headstones and footstones mark the graves of the family elders Charles and Mary Moore (both dead in 1805), three of their children, and a family extended by marriage and birth. Chains encircle the swept and weeded earth to keep visitors from treading on the dead. We read each legible inscription aloud—*Sacred to the Memory of...*—pausing to imagine what once filled weathered gaps. Thrushes and chickadees conversed above us from oak, beech, and sweetgum branches. Then, turning back, we paused. Unnoticed at first, angular rocks spread like stepping-stones beyond the footpath, through an understory tangle of leaf litter and vinca. One . . . two . . . three . . . four . . . I stopped counting at thirty. Two questions choked between my breath and humid air.

Walnut Grove Plantation, in Spartanburg County, is one of South Carolina's heritage sites, a tourist attraction long listed on the U.S. National Register of Historic Places. The restored manor house, outbuildings, and furnishings, in the register's words, "provide a fully documented picture of life, and an example of social history, in upcountry South Carolina prior to 1830. The house itself is considered one of the finest remaining upcountry plantation houses of the period. Built about 1765 by Charles Moore, a Scotch-Irish immigrant . . ."

Restoration and upkeep of the buildings and adjacent grounds of this once large plantation are indeed impressive. Every first weekend of October the Spartanburg County Historical Association hosts its "family-friendly" Festifall here, touted as "the biggest and best living history event in South Carolina." Volunteers in colonial dress demonstrate blacksmithing, quilting, and pewter-smithing. They fire muskets in militia drills and dance to colonial music. Children learn to dip tallow and beeswax candles and to write with quill pens. Festifall's highlight is the reenactment of a skirmish between patriots and British loyalists during the Revolutionary War. (It's rumored that Walnut Grove may have been a rebel recruitment center before the pivotal Battle of Cowpens.)

Our June tour offered no reenactments but it still celebrated patriotic deeds and drama, as well as the daily life of this immigrant Scots-Irish family who built a "self-sufficient farm" on the Carolina frontier. The history as told to us by a courteous and genial docent, a matronly woman, grew mostly from tangible objects of a well-to-do life. The manor house's front "keeping room" contained the Bible box for important papers, kept by the door in case of fire. Rooms featured original furniture, clapboard and paneled walls. Food brought from the kitchen outbuilding was moved from pots to serving dishes in the "changing room." Gardens, grape arbor, and dipping well were beautifully kept. A "hoppin' up block" for entering carriages or mounting horses lay at the end of the front walk. One could easily imagine sitting at the dining table, entering a carriage with graceful step, or otherwise enjoying the hospitality of the Moores.

The smooth-worn handles of a froe and splitting maul and other implements in the outbuildings showed long use. But our guide did not speak of those who used the tools to serve the household or work the land—not until asked. Her only mention was a brief nod that "some fieldstones mark the graves of family slaves."

My queries near tour's end—*Where were the quarters? How many people were enslaved here?*—met polite silence. Was *I* impolite to ask such things? When questioned through another tack what happened here through the 1800s, our guide began, "Oh, do you mean was the manor house ever damaged? Oh no . . ." She then returned to the Battle of Cowpens in 1781, "a great victory for the patriots." History as told to us ended in 1805.

Had we visited another day, had we walked with another guide, perhaps we could have heard of those who labored here in bondage. Walnut Grove's website notes that Mr. Moore "relied on a dozen enslaved African Americans." It also states that the plantation "recounts how free and enslaved people settled the South Carolina Backcountry, fought for independence, and built a new nation."

But on this day Dorinda and I heard nothing. Avoidance lay within gentility and silence as the tour's carefully framed story muted a larger human presence. Walking by so many untended, unnamed graves I felt as if part of me lay beneath fieldstones, buried by a whitewashed past. Those who once owned this land dared to own those forced to work it. It seemed that Walnut Grove's memory was fenced property, too.

I later saw Lesson 22 of Project Discovery, a program offering virtual field trips produced by South Carolina Educational Television with the state's department of education. In this lesson, an "Upstate Visit to Walnut Grove Plantation," children in kindergarten through eighth grade explore colonial life and heroism. "Discovery words" in the lesson guide include *plantation*, "a large estate or farm on which crops are raised, often by resident workers," and *self-sufficient*, "capable of providing for oneself without the help of others." The lesson gives much information on how to make candles—fifty to eighty dips of linen wicks in tallow and beeswax make one candle (on a cold day). But it offers no words on those "resident workers" who somehow weren't yet were "others." Seeing African American children visiting Walnut Grove in the video pricked a memory: I'm asking my fifth-grade social-studies teacher, Mrs. Devlin, if I could become a slave. To that outdoors-loving child the job of a resident worker on a self-sufficient farm would have seemed a wonderful thing.

THE REMEMBERED AND told past. This story's *who* were valorized plantation owners and patriots, the *when* only four decades. What did it matter that words on slavery or those enslaved were absent, or that those buried in more than 120 graves a short walk from the manor house were barely mentioned? Perhaps there is no requirement that a public story must deal with any particular topic. Yet South Carolina was founded on slavery and wresting profit from the land. British planters had brought both the institution and the enslaved from Barbados to the coastal Carolinas in the mid to late 1600s, transplanting both the status of Africans in servitude for life and the assumption that those worked to death could be replaced. Some settlers also encouraged Native trading partners to raid neighboring villages for captives to be shipped to the Indies for profit. By the 1690s South Carolina had codified the most violent denial of the enslaved's rights and legal standing of all Britain's Atlantic colonies. It soon became the only mainland colony with a Black majority, most on low-country rice plantations. Samuel Dyssli, a newcomer in 1737, remarked that

"Carolina looks more like a negro country than like a country settled by white people."

What did it matter that hopes for independence held by enslaved men and women in the southern colonies tended to be recognized by the British during the Revolutionary War? Late in 1775 Lord Dunmore, the departing royal governor of Virginia, promised freedom to all willing to run away and bear arms for His Majesty. George Washington worried if "that man is not crushed by spring, he will become the most formidable enemy America has; his strength will increase as a snow ball by rolling; and faster, if some expedient cannot be hit upon to convince the slaves and servants of the impotency of his designs." At the end of hostilities British ships would carry upwards of twenty thousand "fugitive slaves" fleeing South Carolina and Georgia, perhaps twelve thousand sailing from Charleston Harbor alone. Thousands more men and women of color who had seized their own independence when the war disrupted plantation life still roamed at large, trying to resist planters' attempts to reimpose the old order. Off and on for nearly thirty more years South Carolina would import nearly ninety thousand Africans in chains, half the new state's enslaved population held in the Piedmont upcountry. All of this as Walnut Grove grew to become a three-thousand-acre plantation.

Our tour hasn't ceased to trouble me. The lives of those who remained after Charles and Mary Moore's deaths didn't end in 1805. Neither did their relationships to this Piedmont land. The Moore family kept at least some of the plantation grounds. I knew this because a descendant donated the house and eight acres to the Spartanburg County Foundation in 1961. I wondered what else a little digging could reveal, if some path to those buried in unnamed graves could be found. Of course my reasons were selfish. I needed to answer the hollowness that held me since that June day. Many of my own ancestors, my mother's people, lie in forgotten plantation graves; their lives forgotten, too.

• • •

If there is an *after*, there is also a *before*. The Piedmont, like the Blue Ridge west of it, was assembled by collision and displacement, geological and cultural. The Appalachian Mountains are one part of a long, sutured seam marking the final closing of an ancient ocean basin, the Atlantic's predecessor, that zippered shut hundreds of millions of years ago. Current theories hold that islands and other far-traveled landmasses caught in the middle accreted one after another onto the continent's edge. Then, as always, erosion took over, relentless ever since, to wear crumpled bedrock down into a rolling, hilly upland. Piedmont—"foot of the mountains."

Other collisions occurred here, too. A copy of a 1775 map lies open on my desk as I write: *An Accurate Map Of North And South Carolina, With Their Indian Frontier, Shewing in a distinct manner all the Mountains, Rivers, Swamps, Marshes, Bays, Creeks, Harbours, Sandbanks and Soundings on the Coasts; with The Roads and Indian Paths; as well as The Boundary or Provincial Lines, The Several Townships, and other divisions of the Land In Both The Provinces; the whole From Actual Surveys.* Authored by Henry Mouzon and others, printed in London.

On it the forks of the Tyger River flow southeast as nearly parallel veins from their "Appalachean" headwaters, joining just above the "Path from the Cherokees." My finger traces this path northeast past the "Catawbaw Nation" into North Carolina where many roads converge. I take the path the other way, too, crossing a sharp north-south line that follows no topography. Beyond it lies acknowledged Cherokee land. This line bounded the then northwestern corner of

South Carolina's province, just one instant in the westward advance of Britain's frontier. Looking at later maps I can see the flooding colonial tide.

Several Scots-Irish families, Charles Moore's among them, heeded the Appalachian fabric as they migrated from Pennsylvania to settle South Carolina's backcountry in the early 1760s. They took wagon roads that followed ancestral tribal trails. Down long mountain valleys—the Great Valley, Shenandoah Valley—south and west, before cutting east through a break in the Blue Ridge onto the Piedmont. To them this was land waiting to be claimed; to the Cherokee it was homeland ceded by yet another treaty. I see creek and river names on current topographic maps—Beaverdam, Bear, Wolf, Buffalo, Tyger—hinting at an unfamiliar wildness these colonists found.

Unlike Carolina's low country the upper Piedmont wasn't an easily tilled coastal plain. No large rice plantations would or could claim it. No broad navigable rivers meandered here; bedrock lay too near the surface. The first settlers would choose tracts along the fertile bottomlands of the Tyger branches. The Moores chose well, taking up 550 acres granted by King George III by the north fork. The house they would eventually build stands just east of the river. Walnut Grove.

Lying perhaps two hundred miles from the coastal port of Charleston, barely linked by passable roads in the early years, up-country farms such as theirs had to balance self-sufficiency with any opportunity to satisfy commercial ambitions. Most farms raised livestock: cattle, horses, sheep, and swine. Many as Governor Montagu observed in 1772 were "producing luxuriantly Indigo, Hemp, Tobacco, and all English Grains." Cotton would soon be cultivated in gardens and provision grounds for home-spinning to make cloth.

The Moore family holdings grew by grant and purchase. In 1785, Charles Moore, "yeoman of the one part," deeded land to his eldest son, Thomas, "yeoman of the other part," just west of the river. There, about a mile as the crow flies from Walnut Grove, the son would build Fredonia. One Charleston visitor in 1804 found Thomas Moore and his family living "in the backwoods state, [but] on a more refined scale than that presented by the generality of settlers, his circumstances being more independent."

I turn to another map, this one of the Spartanburgh District surveyed by J. Whitten in 1820 and "improved" for Robert Mills's 1825 atlas of the state of South Carolina. The region has taken shape in the intervening half century. Greenville and Laurens districts lie to the west, not acknowledged Cherokee land. A dozen or so roads converge on the village of Spartanburgh in the district's center. "Poor land" is inked in many places north of the village; the Tyger River forks meander south of it. Walnut Grove doesn't appear, but Fredonia does. So do occasional iron works, cotton factories, and nearly fifty mills powered by flowing water.

I pause over Whitten's map to take in how this Piedmont landscape and its yeoman society changed in the years since the Revolution. Long-strand cotton so common in coastal lowlands didn't grow well here. Shorter strand varieties could, but sticky seeds clung to fibers. A new gin capable of plucking out these seeds opened the way for cotton to become a staple crop grown for export and profit. New Englanders came south to build the first upcountry cotton mills, on the Tyger River forks, between 1816 and 1818. Streams that couldn't carry large vessels could power factories. The Piedmont thus assumed a new value as a landscape of market cultivation. So did those captive laborers who planted seeds and picked bolls.

South Carolina's yearly cotton exports soared from less than ten thousand pounds in 1790 to six million pounds just a decade later, the greatest yield from the Piedmont. Within twenty years, from 1790 to 1810, the number of enslaved persons in the upcountry would triple as plantation fields grew in size and number. And at least one northern transplant, a cotton factory owner, would soon choose to depart. "I wish to leave this part of the country and wish to settle myself and family in a free state," Rhode Island native Philip Weaver explained, "where myself and family will not be looked down upon with contempt because I am opposed to the abominable practice of slavery."

All of this comes from easily accessible sources. Scholarly references on South Carolina's colonial settlement and early state history. Maps available online from the Library of Congress. Walnut Grove's website. Charles Moore's will and estate inventory also found online. The deed from father to eldest son in the first three pages of Spartanburg's Deed Book A. Various histories of Spartanburg County, one of them dedicated "to the Confederate heroes, both living and dead." But in this scattered "evidence" I cannot find the strata of lives deposited near the Tyger River's north fork, the lives of those enslaved on this land. The view is telescoped and shadowed at best. Though tempted to learn if African American Moores live in the area today, to contact them and ask about their history, I stop. A line of privacy would be crossed—I don't want to trespass unwanted. Instead I would continue to search public and published records, turning next to the U.S. Federal Census.

The first census in 1790 lists both Charles and eldest son Thomas as heads of households with human property. Each succeeding decadal glimpse counts generations of white Moores who lived by the North Tyger River. Run together, these instants suggest an arc of a prominent family of education and growing means, a family that tended to own more property than most of its neighbors. In 1800, five years before his death, Charles Moore held twelve "slaves"; his oldest son, eleven. The three sons, Thomas, Andrew Barry, and Charles Jr., held between them nearly fifty people enslaved ten years later. By 1830 it appears that only Dr. Andrew Barry Moore—a Dickinson College schoolmate of Roger B. Taney who as Supreme

Court chief justice would rule in the Dred Scott case—still lived on family land at Fredonia, homeplace for years to come. Censuses before his death in 1848 count more than forty "slaves" in his possession. Dr. Moore left nearly three thousand acres to his widow, Nancy, and their three children. The family had become substantial upcountry planters, cultivating hills and valley alluvium on a large scale for the upper Piedmont.

1860. The year of the last census with a "slave schedule," the last view of what cotton and slavery made of this country. Four months before South Carolina seceded from the Union, the assistant marshal noted fifty "slave inhabitants" between Nancy Moore and her elder son, Andrew Charles Moore. Their combined real estate was valued at more than twenty thousand dollars; their combined personal estates, including those "inhabitants" so counted, estimated at just under sixty thousand dollars. These figures do not count the holdings of Nancy Moore's son-in-law, Samuel Means, who held his wife's interests.

What these numbers mean. Fewer than one-third of Spartanburg area families "owned" any human beings as chattel in 1860. Of those who did the average holding was eight or nine people. Half the area's farmers cultivated less than one hundred acres. Perhaps half of those growing cotton barely made a single bale. Yet, young Andrew C. Moore, writing to his mother from the University of Virginia early in 1860, asks her to verify if his fields produced thirty-nine or forty bales. A Mr. Thomas Hill, overseer, is enumerated on the census with family members.

At the edge of Civil War I'm still little closer to the lives of those who worked this land. Census "data" privilege property owners, the ones who could declare themselves, by law and custom, heads of households. Individual "holdings" listed on a "slave schedule" can't even hint at how those enslaved and free on a plantation negotiated circles of intimacy and of discord.

*

I TURN TO the 1870 census. More has happened in the past decade than perhaps any other, certainly more than I can imagine. The Moore land lies in an area called Fair Forest Township. Those who appeared only as numbers inventoried by age and sex in 1860 have names entered five years after war's end. Those alive who stayed, that is. They are heads of households. Farmers. Wives "keeping house." Domestic servants. Many have large families. Some have the surnames of prominent white families. Wofford, Means, Moore.

I notice something else. No African American owns land in Fair Forest Township. I scan page after page. The "value of real estate" column lies blank for each one, though most white families there also appear to rent farms. What land that is owned tends to be worth less than two thousand dollars, most farms ranging in the low to mid-hundreds. Yet two families stand out. The real estate of Thomas John Moore, the younger son who survived the war, and his brother-in-law Samuel Means is valued, respectively, at fifteen thousand and twenty-two thousand dollars.

April 1865 was a threshold. I want to know how the conflict's outcome played out on this soil, how it might have contributed to public silences today. A hint is offered by a "labor and commodity inventory" of Thomas Moore's lands in 1866, which was compiled by a descendant and published by his son in 2009. The inventory draws from a plantation ledger book and the memories of one Benjamin Moore, an African American whose parents long served the family. Scores of hands worked in fields owned by Thomas Moore and held by his brother-in-law: the Upper Place, Home Place (Fredonia), Middle Place, and Lower Place (Walnut Grove). A labor contract adds another clue. Thomas John Moore, "the party of the first part" has the privilege "to appropriate to himself enough of the share of the crops of the party of the second part [freedmen] at the time they

are gathered to satisfy all demands he may have against them. . . ."
Should the party of the second part "become offensive," Moore
could "dispossess them of his property in their hands and expel
them summarily from the place without compensation."

I don't know how many times I've reread these words: "dispossess them of *his* property in *their* hands and expel them." It's impossible for me to know whether Thomas Moore ever dispossessed or
expelled anyone from these lands by the North Tyger River. I can
imagine, though, that the threat of losing the soil one had tilled
perhaps in all memory, of not being able to claim it, was threat of
a breath withheld.

In 1870 no African American owned land in Fair Forest. At the
turn of the twentieth century only five of more than two hundred
African American families in the township own farms. I count ten
more on the census pages who have farms mortgaged. Two of the
fifteen are named Moore. Numa Moore Sr. worked the white Moore
lands for decades. Now, in 1900, his son Numa Jr. and his family
work to own a farm. Benjamin Moore, literate like his father, owns
a farm outright with his wife. His father and mother don't. By far
most Black families in the township either share-crop, have tenancy
agreements, or work as laborers.

I pause again at the 1910 census, which now calls the local township Walnut Grove. Changes in fortune for good or ill mark each
decade, the circumstances of in-between years hidden from view.
Benjamin Moore still owns his farm. Numa Moore Jr. is dead. His
widow, Salena (or Selina or Celina—it depends on the census),
owns no land. There is no mortgage. Now a woman in her forties,
literate, enumerated as "mulatto," she rents with her eight children
perhaps the same fields they'd worked to make theirs. Ten years later
Selina lives with five of her children in the town of Spartanburg.
They rent a house on Clement Street, south of Main, in a community established by freedmen and women after the Civil War. She

and her elder daughter cook for white families; another daughter works as a house servant. They own no land or home. Here I stop, having intruded unasked into this woman's private hardship. No matter that it's after the fact. Each census is an enumerated instant giving little context or detail on the lives of these people or on their felt ties to place. What *is* clear is that into the twentieth century very few African American families came to possess land as their own property. I've wondered what deeper forms of possession, more concrete and felt, they had. Not finding their stories doesn't mean they never existed. Spoken words, exhaled breath, are to me just as real as paper records. So is soil embedded into one's palms. Or knowing the seasonal movements of hawks and salamanders. This Piedmont land and its societies, a measure of their known world, also bounded it. I now needed to know—for it had become an obsession—how the currents of Reconstruction and Redemption had entrained and deposited the "emancipated" in Spartanburg County.

So I learn that South Carolina rushed to enact a Black Code after laying down arms in 1865, a code forbidding African Americans from any occupation besides farmer or servant, unless they paid a tax and received a special license. The code required labor contracts ordering work from sunup to sundown, from "can see to can't." Laborers couldn't leave plantations or invite visitors without permission of the landowner. None could own firearms or join a militia. Freedmen without jobs became "vagrants" subject to the law. When the military administrator of the Carolinas during Reconstruction, a former Union general, suspended the code, Spartanburg's white citizenry became incensed. To them this was essential legislation.

And the most extreme resistance to federal Reconstruction took place in upcountry South Carolina, where a powerful "combination" calling itself the Ku Klux Klan thwarted the Fourteenth and Fifteenth amendments with great ardor. With the 1868 elections night riders intimidated, whipped, and murdered members of Lincoln's party. Freedmen were dissuaded from voting. Still, Republicans carried the upcountry in the 1870 elections, perhaps in large part because the Reconstruction governor had organized and armed a Black militia. The Klan responded by mounting a campaign of brutal violence that grew to an unprecedented scale. Spartanburg became one of the most eruptive of the Piedmont counties with its white Democratic majority. Klansmen terrorized anyone thought to have crossed the line of proper race relations or who refused to bow to the region's honored "property and intelligence." Beaten or turned off their land were freed people, white Republicans, wartime Unionists, and scalawags. Spartanburg's first Black magistrate was lynched. "These combinations embrace at least two-thirds of the active white men of those counties," the U.S. attorney general advised President Grant, "and have the sympathy and countenance of a majority of the one-third." Local courts disregarded "nigger" evidence of criminal acts. Many a Black man was charged and imprisoned on no evidence at all. As one Spartanburg farmer put it, "a heap goes to the penotensuary & all that is convicted for stealing is done voting."

So dire had the situation become that, in the autumn of 1871, the president suspended the writ of habeas corpus and declared nine Piedmont counties, Spartanburg among them, in a "condition of lawlessness." Federal troops made mass arrests, but few Klan leaders would be convicted. Still, some scholars have called these trials the federal government's most concerted attempt to enforce the political and civil rights of freemen and freedmen.

AFRICAN AMERICANS TILLED white-owned Spartanburg soil in 1800 and in 1870. Most of those who stayed in the area would do so half a century later, all the while trying to shape their own lives on the land. I wanted there to be some remove granted by time. That much had changed in the last century, even though the grand dragon of South Carolina's Klan for most of the 1960s lived in Spartanburg County. Even though, in the name of "urban renewal," the city of Spartanburg razed the century-old Southside community. Families once enslaved had made homes there at the end of Liberty Street following the war. This is where Selina Moore moved her family after leaving land they'd never own. One line in the city's 1970 renewal proposal for federal funding reads, "No historical areas are involved in the project activities."

That same year the National Register of Historic Places, the official list of "the nation's historic places worthy of preservation," included Walnut Grove Plantation. Fredonia was listed shortly thereafter but removed after the house burned down. Walnut Grove today preserves about sixty acres. Dorman High School occupies the old Upper Place. Interstate 26 slices through the holdings, paralleling the North Tyger River on its way to Columbia. Woods have reclaimed much of the land. Subdivisions like Moore's Crossing and King's Grant claim even more.

· · ·

Months after visiting Walnut Grove I stood in the oldest burying ground of Deerfield, at the edge of a wooded terrace near my home in western Massachusetts. Around 1670 Puritan colonists surveyed and claimed this site above the floodplain of a river they'd call by the same name. For several decades Deerfield would be colonial New England's northwesternmost frontier settlement. If I had any illusions that the told and untold stories from Spartanburg, the properties of desire, were unique to the South, they ended here.

Deerfield shares elements of its origin with Piedmont, South Carolina. It, too, lies within Appalachian terrain, its deep geologic past and more recent human history also entailing collision, displacement, and erosion. Colonists settled on traditional Wôbanaki (Abenaki/Pocumtuck) homelands, encountering not primeval forests but an existing village site. The land had already been burned and cleared for planting fields, meadows, glades.

The colonial village, with wood-frame houses lining a mile-long main street, still retains the original plan and scale. It became a registered National Historic Landmark in 1962. According to promotional materials, Historic Deerfield "is an outdoor history museum that focuses on the history and culture of the Connecticut River Valley and early New England. It has a dual mission of educating the public about the lifestyles of the diverse people who lived here long ago and of preserving antique buildings and collections of regional furniture, silver, textiles, and other decorative arts." With the Flynt Center for Early New England Life and twelve furnished main-street houses built between 1730 and 1850, Historic Deerfield displays more than twenty-five thousand objects made or used in these years.

The regular season opens with a Patriot's Day Revolutionary Muster and Parade in mid to late April. Visitors watch open-hearth cooking and powder horn carving. They learn about the "shot heard 'round the world" that began the Revolutionary War. They "experience" a day at a training encampment, with an artillery and musket drill firing black powder. Historic Deerfield offers many other programs over the year for families and children's groups. One can practice writing with quill pens, learn about blacksmithing or growing heirloom vegetables, or see how flax is dressed and turned into cloth.

What had not been part of Historic Deerfield's public story until recently is the long presence of people of African ancestry who helped build the community. Most but not all of them were held in bondage from the earliest days to years after the Revolution, when slavery came to a slow ragged end in the new state of Massachusetts. I learned of this part of Deerfield's past not at the museum but on a walk through the town with a retired Amherst College physics professor.

Robert Romer had volunteered as a guide in one of the historic houses. There he found out about Jenny Cole, her son Cato, and Titus, who were held by Reverend Jonathan Ashley, Deerfield's minister from 1732 until his death in 1780. Bob then researched the entire town, reading wills, estate inventories, bills of sale, account books, minister notes, and church records. He learned that between one-third to half the households held people enslaved on the eve of the Revolution. Other residents bartered for or hired their labor—to clear land, to plow and reap, to milk cows and kill hogs, to dress flax and make brooms, to build houses and to dig graves. Reverend Ashley justified servitude by preaching that "such as are by Divine providence placed in the State of Servants, are not excluded from Salvation, but may become the Lord's freemen" and "if you are Christ's freemen you may contentedly be servants in the world."

Until the last few years little had publicly acknowledged Deerfield's residents of African descent beyond an 1895 town history whose author chose in his words to "face the facts." Of three centuries of stone markers at the burying ground, not one is known to stand over the grave of an African American.

I soon understood that desire also brought slavery and the enslaved to colonial New England in more than one way. The Massachusetts Bay Colony was the first of the English colonies to sanction the institution legally. In 1641 Puritan colonists codified in the Massachusetts Body of Liberties a guarantee of their own and a willingness to take those of captives, strangers, and criminals: "There shall never be any bond-slavery, villenage or captivitie amongst us; unless it be lawfull captives taken in just warrs, and such strangers as willingly sell themselves, or are solde to us. . . ." Captivity in a "just warr" began with the 1637 war made on the Pequots. Some survivors were shipped aboard the Salem vessel *Desire* to the Puritan colony on Providence Island in the Caribbean. The *Desire* returned in 1638 with what Governor John Winthrop called a cargo of "cotton and tobacco and negroes &c." The "negroes," already held as "perpetual servants" on Providence Island, came in exchange for Pequot captives.

With its holds partitioned into racks two feet by six feet, with leg irons and bars, the *Desire* may be the first documented "slave ship" *from* the English mainland colonies. And Emanuel Downing outlined what may be the oldest-known written argument for the slave trade on the mainland. In a 1645 letter to Winthrop, his brother-in-law, he proposed how profit could be gained in a war with the Narragansett people:

> If upon a Just warre the Lord should deliver them into our hands, wee might easily have men woemen and children enough to exchange for Moores, which wilbe more gayneful pilladge for us then wee conceive, for I doe not see how wee can thrive untill wee get into a stock of slaves sufficient to doe all our buisiness. . . . And I suppose you know verie well how wee shall mayneteyne 20 Moores cheaper then one Englishe servant.

Puritan New England was as implicated as South Carolina. The needs of island sugar plantations for regular supplies of food and materials drove much of the north's commercial economy. By the start of the Revolution perhaps two-thirds to four-fifths of New England's exports—timber, barrels, livestock, dried fish, corn, wheat, potatoes, onions, flour, more—were Caribbean bound. Ships returned with harvested sugar, molasses, and other island products. From that molasses distilleries produced rum, much of it traded in Africa for captives. Rhode Island and Massachusetts distillers were particularly ambitious. While slavery's scale in New England never reached that of the South, Northern colonists just as firmly accepted the idea, the practice, and its profits. And those seized and held as servants for life, though fewer in number, still felt the confining blow of forced bondage.

"TO A LARGE degree it may be said that Americans bought their independence with slave labor," historian Edmund Morgan once observed. "The paradox is American, and it behooves Americans to understand it if they would understand themselves." I remember grade-school lessons: tobacco, rice, sugar, and cotton produced on such a scale by Southern plantations that owners sold them on markets overseas. But what wasn't taught was how slavery's yield drove the economies of all thirteen colonies. How it then scaffolded the new nation's infrastructure even in regions where coerced servitude had ended. Just as the products of slavery were an ultimate source of eighteenth-century New England's commercial economy, so, too, were they in the antebellum North when the cotton trade reigned and New England ran myriad textile mills. "Cotton thread holds the union together," Ralph Waldo Emerson wrote in his journal on May 23, 1846. "Patriotism for holidays and summer evenings, with music and rockets, but cotton thread is the Union."

A supposed "sectional" economy stitched South Carolina to Massachusetts, the nation to Africa, Europe, the Caribbean, and the rest of the Americas. Such that New York City grew as the cotton trade's financial center and a major port. Southern plantation-grown cotton was so much the root of New York City's wealth that in January 1861, the eve of Civil War, mayor Fernando Wood urged the city's secession from the Union: "With our aggrieved brethren of the Slave States, we have friendly relations and a common sympathy."

The privilege and profits slavery afforded reside not only in the past. Major American financial institutions, newspapers, schools, as well as tobacco, textile, and railroad companies amassed wealth or were otherwise supported by slavery's financial gains. Two predecessor banks of JPMorgan Chase used thousands of captive Africans as collateral on loans to plantation owners, even taking possession of more than a thousand human beings. The founders of Brown Brothers Harriman & Co. built the country's oldest and largest partnership bank by lending to Southern planters, brokering crops, and investing in the South's financial system. Aetna and other companies wrote life insurance policies on human "property." Wealthy enslavers and traders were among the original benefactors of elite educational institutions, Brown, Harvard, and Yale universities among them.

• • •

What to remember, what to forget. Colonial historian Bernard Bailyn writes that memory's "relation to the past is an embrace. It is not a critical, skeptical reconstruction of what happened. It is the spontaneous, unquestioned experience of the past. It is absolute, not tentative or distant, and it is expressed in signs and signals, symbols, images, and mnemonic clues of all sorts. It shapes our awareness whether we know it or not, and it is ultimately emotional, not intellectual." How a society remembers can't be separated from how it wants to be remembered or from what it wishes it was—that is, if we believe stories of ancestors reflect who we are and how we came to be. The past is remembered and told by desire.

Heritage tourism has become one of the most popular sectors of travel and tourism in the country. It's a key "industry" for both South Carolina and Massachusetts. Our tour at Walnut Grove celebrated the founding of a nation. Historical memory anchored a patriotic identity *in* place, for South Carolina claims more Revolutionary War battles fought on its soil than any other state. Visitors participating in Festifall can see themselves as part of this heritage of independence. Visitors to Deerfield's Patriot's Day can as well. Who wouldn't desire a celebratory and uplifting story of origins?

Some time after my visit to Walnut Grove, I spoke with the then director of the Spartanburg County Historical Association, which administers the plantation. She reminded me of how public history sites work. "You can't tell everything," she said. "You have to decide what is most relevant, what the site can illustrate best." Besides, I was told, apparently few documentary records of how Walnut Grove's lands were used through the nineteenth century were available. "It's important to avoid speculation," she added.

This makes sense, and yet . . . silence has reinforced a status quo that continues to privilege what's always been privileged in popular history. For without acknowledging what binds the past to the present, narratives such as that told to Dorinda and me can appear safely resolved and innocent. In its focus on a War for Independence and beginnings, on a few specific heroes and landowners, the told story lies remote from a later war of upheaval and endings. Patriotic unity, not nineteenth-century discord.

I've found few plantation or colonial attractions, north or south, that honestly acknowledge the presence and contributions of African Americans. Offerings of "the American experience" often exclude slavery and its aftermath, or they present stories that are uncritical or unquestioning of convention. One can still find sentimentalized images of "moonlight and magnolias" and "contented slaves." Perhaps worse are the false facades that appear to present slavery to the public but instead empty it of substance and meaning.

Consider the last "discovery activity" of Lesson 22's virtual field trip to Walnut Grove: "A plantation requires that many people work together to be a self-sustaining unit. Some of these workers include carpenters, cooks, stable hands, butlers, field workers, blacksmiths, housekeepers, and seamstress[es]." The lesson asks students "to write 'a day in the life' journal entries from the different perspectives of these workers." This could appear to be benign teaching until one remembers that South Carolina law made it a crime to teach the enslaved to read or write. Even with exceptions, which occurred on the Moores' land, the general rule was to forbid such "mental stimulation."

Celebratory lessons and stories that don't face ambiguity and complexity might seem to exempt us from needing to look more closely. Perhaps this is possible if a Southern plantation really was only "a large estate or farm on which crops are raised, often by resident workers." Yet such told history makes it easier to disregard the enslavement of millions. Or, if slavery did happen, it wasn't so bad. Or it was just a temporary anomaly corrected long ago. There remains no public agreement on slavery's impact, trauma, or human costs. I still hear passionate arguments that people of African heritage should be grateful for the better and more civilized life chattel bondage gave their ancestors in this "white" nation. I still see slavery trivialized for entertainment. In the early 1990s, plans for the proposed Disney's America historical theme park included exhibits on slavery that designers guaranteed to be "painful, disturbing, and agonizing" to tourists. The project was canceled amid widespread controversy.

A supposedly long-gone past offers an illusory comfort to the living. *It's not my fault. I wasn't there. I didn't own any slaves, and neither did my family.* Barricaded safely in the present, the living can even condemn the institution while ignoring what made it desirable to privileged classes—and what has fed an ever-mutable caste system to the present.

HISTORY AS TAUGHT to me in grade school tried to box all that is known of a fixed past into a universal, sequential story. A story that was innocent, independent, impelled. A story beyond human manipulation. The historian's job was simply to retrieve then reveal the securely passed past, waiting in storage. But that sense of history neglects our relationships to each other and to what is "known" and "not known" of the past. How and why do we know what we know? Who is doing the (re)collecting then telling? What I think of as history on this land—the events that occurred *and* the narratives told of them—can never be complete or single-voiced. Each of us participates in it. We contribute to it as players, as witnesses, as narrators, as producers and consumers, in an ongoing past-to-present.

What to remember, what to forget? Perhaps no recorded "fact" can stand innocent. Each told fact holds meaning to the recorder, and each historical narrative (re)presents accidental and deliberate silences or omissions. I've tried to imagine the countless *why*s behind recordings and forgettings across two centuries—all the successive moments of then to now—as each generation with the power of accepted voice presumed to define legitimate values, language, and terms of debate. *This is the way things were. This is the way things had to be. Here is where history happened.* But power of voice doesn't mean the voices of all.

The silence of Walnut Grove's burying grounds seemed to belie the enslaver's power to extract work without consent from the enslaved. Not just work, but blood, breath, life itself. Silence reminded me, too, of pieces erased from a many-storied past: complex communities excised, interior lives of "property-in-person" ignored.

Yet those forced to work Piedmont soil had an intimate, immediate relationship with this land, cultivating and harvesting its yield by hand. Another yield had to be a community geography apart from the planters' lives and imposed bondage. Private and communal meanings, elements of self-autonomy and agency, emerged from endurance and strength grown *in* place. Hunting and growing gardens could enlarge both means and knowledge of subsistence; uncultivated nature beyond the cotton fields could provide food, medicine, sanctuary. But that landscape is and isn't there. The physical terrain may roughly remain, but secret paths, symbolic networks for navigating one's way, and any shared ways of defining or making sense of their known world linger as ghosts. That landscape's fabric, its vitality and dailiness, left little physical expression to those not taught to see.

And after the war, freed men and women negotiated narrow frames of sharecropping, tenancy, and Jim Crow. To "dispossess them of his property in their hands" always a threat. Only a few African Americans would come to own small farms near Walnut Grove by the turn of the twentieth century. The power to define public memory, to select sites anchoring it, would also remain largely in the hands of those who possessed the land—Spartanburg's "property and intelligence" and their descendants. The power to segregate people under Jim Crow and to segregate memory would work in concert. There are those who might even argue that long-dead enslavers still maintained a form of possession and control.

THAT INHABITING THE same time, sharing a past, doesn't mean sharing common experiences or points of view was never clearer than on the tour of Walnut Grove. We live among countless landscapes of memory in this country. They convey both remembrance and omission, privileging particular arcs of story while neglecting so many others. Historical sites are contested "story-sites" for the meanings of America's past-to-present.

To whom and what is history responsible? What I realized at the burying grounds was that each of us is implicated in locating the past-to-present. As I might dig through earth and time to open a grave, the task is to uncover the strata of obscuring language and acts, of meanings shrouded over generations. The question had to be turned around and made personal: What then is *my* relationship with history, told and untold, on this land?

I've not yet found the antebellum lives of my mother's people beyond an estate inventory from Marengo County, Alabama. But I've come closer to understanding why I don't know about them, why Momma told me nothing, why silence is residue of memory's erosion. Ancestors disappeared—into paper records of property rather than human lives remembered in story, into a plantation owner's surname, into graves unmarked or forgotten long ago.

It is hard to engage painful elements of America's past and be self-reflective, particularly if one must confront deeply ingrained beliefs and ideas that have shaped, or made comfortable, one's sense of self or place. Or if one seeks to shed a sense of inherited shame or pain in order to step away from stories of group victimization. But the legacy of slavery, and the racism it fed and reinforced, remains a malignant symbiosis. It feeds who we Americans think we are, as citizens and as communities. It still festers as untended wounds, quite open and disfiguring to some, hidden from view to others.

I don't have answers but I do have desires. That the intricate relations implicating us in each other's lives could be acknowledged by recent immigrant and native, by descendant of colonists and those enslaved by colonists. This isn't being trapped by history or consumed by guilt over the past, nor is it being victim without end. It is instead honoring the lives of those so often unacknowledged by taking responsibility for the past-in-present—by opposing injustices today for which accountability of the living is direct. This comes closest in my mind to a true *re*-pairing toward truth and reconciliation.

After hollowness what I felt most acutely at Walnut Grove and Deerfield's burying grounds was a life-hunger for relation. I'd withered far too much in what Audre Lorde called "the learned tolerance of deprivation of each other."

MIGRATING IN A BORDERED LAND

From the front cockpit of this Great Lakes biplane, the surrounding mountains and broad plain below seemed familiar. I couldn't remember ever setting foot there, yet I knew the place. After the pilot handed me the control and I turned the plane into evening sun, memory returned. This was Texas! It was Oklahoma and Kansas. Hollywood's versions, that is. *Red River. Oklahoma!* How many times had I watched Montgomery Clift and John Wayne ride in this same light? That was the child-me searching for home in every possible western image, even mythical Old Wests. Now, less than an hour to sunset, slant light shaped the swells and hollows of the Canelo Hills and Sonoita Plain. The Huachuca, Mustang, and Whetstone Mountains blushed for a rose-tinged instant. Beyond them, to the east, the San Pedro River's dark, winding course settled into dusk. No visible line separated Mexico from the United States, Sonora from Arizona. Land and sky stretched to the horizon.

Southeastern Arizona's borderlands had drawn me for sharp-edged reasons that long eluded words. My mother had come here, too, in her youth as an army nurse stationed at Fort Huachuca and the prisoner-of-war camp at Florence. That was in the last years of the Second World War. A lifetime ago—a decade before meeting my father, nearly two decades before my birth. That was when Fort Huachuca was Arizona's third-largest city.

"Why do you want to go there?" were Momma's only words to me before my first visit. I'd suspected that the place had marked her, so quiet was she about this past. I populated her silences, beyond "I learned to bowl there," with imagined stories. Such that a statement my mother would repeat on occasion in her pointed and precise diction, "I am not a race, I am a human being," could (in my mind) hold within its web of origins one filament extending back to Fort Huachuca and Florence. I suppose this as much as anything was why I'd come—at first.

Arizona is in the news as I write these words. Continuing repercussions from the Supreme Court's split decision on S.B. 1070, the state's immigration law. Continuing impacts of the multiyear ban on teaching ethnic studies in Tucson schools. Borders erected here long ago—borders of history, of possession, of meaning—still seem sharp and unyielding. They cut.

My mother came to the San Pedro Valley as part of a massive but little recognized migration and containment. But migratings and borderings of many sorts have always occurred here, where a small river runs through a dry land.

To understand this place, I had to search a deep past of edges and motion. These stories lead to my mother's, and to mine.

SANTA RITA AND Patagonia Mountains. Sonoita Plain, Canelo Hills, San Rafael Valley. Whetstone, Mustang, Huachuca Mountains. San Pedro Valley. Mule and Dragoon Mountains. Sulphur Springs Valley. Chiricahua Mountains. Elongate lithic compasses stand high above valleys collecting their eroded debris. West to east these are southeastern Arizona's offering to the Basin and Range Province.

I stand in the San Pedro Valley, at one of North America's "Last Great Places" according to *LIFE* magazine and The Nature Conservancy. Elevation four thousand feet. To the west and east rise the Huachuca and Mule ranges. Big sacaton grasses bend above my head in a welcome breeze. If not for the winding strip of riparian green, I could be adrift in a grassland sea between mountain archipelagos.

An eastern eye accustomed to large waterways might scoff at a modest stream one can wade and jump across. But the San Pedro River is a vital oasis in an otherwise parched land, one of the last undammed rivers in the American Southwest. Heading near Cananea, Sonora, this fluvial migrant crosses the international border fifteen miles south of where I am to meander northward to its confluence with the Gila River.

The main channel and its tributaries water both overland and aerial routes. Species converge along these dendritic crossroads, among the most biologically diverse areas of the continent.

Gray hawk. Elegant trogon. Lazuli bunting. Broad-billed hummingbird. Vermilion flycatcher. Yellow-billed cuckoo. Birds I'd only imagined I see here. Millions of flyers, hundreds of species take to this avian highway each year, migrating between summer breeding grounds as far north as Canada and wintering grounds in Mexico and Central America. Others choose to nest here, many of them tropical visitors at their farthest reach. By some counts nearly half the bird species in North America make use of the San Pedro, prompting the American Bird Conservancy to name the corridor its first "Globally Important Bird Area" in the United States. But not only birds come—record numbers of mammal, butterfly, reptile, and amphibian species also make use of the valley and flanking mountains. It's not unheard of to glimpse jaguar (*el tigre*), ocelot, and coatimundi roaming about. Sky islands like the Huachuca Mountains are stepping-stones to the tropics.

Yet the river is threatened. Volunteers organized by The Nature Conservancy have wet-dry mapped its course north of the border every June since 1999. Noting where water flows in the channel and where it disappears, their yearly snapshots reveal a river drying. Its once perennial base flow dwindles as Fort Huachuca, the region's largest employer, and the adjacent city Sierra Vista draw from the basin-fill aquifer. A lifeline drained.

I've found shade under cottonwoods and willows by a still-flowing stretch. People pass by, mostly couples with their binoculars prominent. Some migrations, it seems, matter a great deal; some gatherings of diverse lives are a cause for wonder, celebration, or concern. So much so that parts of the watershed were set aside. Congress designated nearly fifty-seven thousand acres north of the international border as the San Pedro Riparian National Conservation Area in 1988. Most comes from two old Mexican land grants, the San Rafael del Valle and San Juan de las Boquillas y Nogales. A few years earlier, about twenty thousand acres of a downstream tributary became Aravaipa Canyon Wilderness. The Bureau of Land Management administers both areas. The Nature Conservancy and Audubon Society also manage land in the watershed. Birders flocking to these avian meccas add to the pressure on fragile habitats.

I follow the channel's flow. This valley and river have been a lifeline to human beings as well—a gathering place of many peoples, a migratory path and a destination for millennia. Here, too, is a border(ed) land.

· · ·

Remains of ancient villages and irrigation networks dot the San Pedro Valley. Petroglyphs and pictographs peer out from rock faces and caves. Worn trails criss-cross the basin and flanking ranges. Ancestors of Hopi, Zuni, Tohono O'odham, and Western Apache peoples left these memory traces. Their narrative traditions, as offered by tribal elders in the San Pedro Ethnohistory Project, emphasize dynamic movement. Traveling. Coming together. Dispersing. Trading goods, customs, and language. Intermarrying. Migrating to, through, and from the San Pedro Valley is central to all.

When the Hisatsinom, ancient ones honored as Hopi ancestors, entered the Fourth World, they began their journeys to the Earth center at Hopi Mesas in different groups of clans. Hopi advisors to the project relate that each clan was guided by a covenant with Màasaw, guardian of Earth, who told them *Ang Kuktota*—"Along there, make footprints." Ancestors didn't travel in linear or one-way paths but gathered from all directions to become Hopi at the mesas. They followed circuitous or spiraling routes through many landscapes. They encountered diverse peoples along the way. Each clan brought experiences, stories, borrowed elements of languages, names, and traditions unique to its migration path. The ways to Hopi Mesas entailed senses of becoming as well as movement across terrain and time.

Tribal participants in the ethnohistory project "repositioned" ancient sites, ruins, and artifacts in the San Pedro Valley as traces of the past left in the land, as part of the land itself. Tohono O'odham *wi'ikam*, things left behind. Zuni "memory pieces." Hopi *itaakuku*, or footprints.

For the Ndee or Ndeh, as the Western Apache know themselves, place-names hold a deep intimacy. Even though generations have lived on reservations to the north, names for the San Pedro Valley and neighboring mountains signal their importance to forebears who lived by the rhythm of seasonal ripenings. Dzì Dasts'án, Wild Grape Mountain. Nadnlid Cho, Big Sunflower Hill. Tûdotł'ish Sikán, Blue Water Pool. To speak place-names is to evoke speech and breath of ancestors. To speak place-names is to remember relationships of survivance. Rigid geopolitical structures that bound reservations stand in stark contrast.

Footprints. Memory pieces. Things left behind. I am not of the Ndee or Hopi or O'odham, yet I know that more than wishful thinking or imagined stories brought me to the San Pedro Valley. This long-contested place witnessed other migrations, by choice and by force, over centuries. Each one crossing borders between myth, history, and lived experience. Each one implicated in and by what had gone before. In tracing them, in assembling fragments of this land's past, I sought what marked my mother—and what of herself she might have left behind.

· · ·

La frontera norteña de Nueva España shifted farther north in 1540 with Francisco Vásquez de Coronado's *entrada*. In search of Cíbola, the legendary cities of gold, his expedition of nearly two thousand—soldiers, priests, servants, enslaved laborers, and Native allies—entered what are now Arizona and New Mexico. But what route did they take across mountainous and arid terrain, *un despoblado*? The expedition certainly required water and forage. The Río Nexpa that they followed may be the San Pedro. Some have suggested a path to the west, perhaps along the Santa Cruz River, which flows by Nogales. Others have looked east. The National Park Service favors the San Pedro Valley.

Coronado National Memorial covers nearly five thousand acres of the southern Huachuca Mountains by the international border. By 7:30 a.m., I had climbed above grass and mesquite scrub through oak, piñon, juniper, sycamore, and walnut woodlands to reach Montezuma Pass at 6,575 feet. The last switchback offered a familiar vista of San Jose Peak rising above the Sonoran skyline in morning light. But unlike earlier visits I also saw a thick dark line bisecting the middle ground, a Sharpie straight-edged with little concern for terrain.

Ah, the new wall . . .

From the pass I could get a quiet overview of the Patagonia Mountains about twenty-five miles to the west, across the San Rafael Valley, over these Huachuca ridges, and across the San Pedro Valley to the east. Four Border Patrol trucks passed me outside of the memorial, but I'd seen no cars the last half hour. Maybe it was still early enough for the pass to be mine.

But five Border Patrol trucks sit parked at the overlook, a large one with what looks like a huge camera rotating on a column mounted on its bed. No one is in sight. A canyon wren whistles from a downslope crevice. With my eyes closed, the wren's cascade seems the only real presence.

At length a truck door opens. The agent, a young African American man, approaches and introduces himself as James. He is friendly, talkative.

"Yes, that's a camera. It rotates 360 degrees and can detect movement within a ten-mile range." He adds that the border fence west of the Huachuca Mountains toward Patagonia is waist-high or lower in places. "It'll stop vehicles from crossing, but not them walking. That's why we have the F-O-B."

"FOB?"

James laughs. "Forward operating base. See that white knob down there?" he says, pointing down the western slope to forest service land. "My shift begins at ten but we're up here because it's the only place nearby with Internet access."

All this through the canyon wren's persistent trill.

My first encounter with the Border Patrol a few years earlier wasn't like this. That morning three patrol trucks had passed me as I drove north from the San Rafael Valley toward Canelo. The fourth truck to pass spun around, coming alongside before I had time to register sunglasses, a hand gesture, or lips mouthing "pull over" as his larger vehicle nudged my car to the road's edge. That man was young, too, in an ironed uniform, RAMIREZ (I think) on the name tag. He walked slowly past my car trunk, taking in the backseat and floor before starting to address me in memorized words and tone. Then a pause, once he really saw me, eyebrows lifting. Whatever he began to say ended with "oh." Still he insisted on checking my trunk and identification. His "Have a good day" ended a five-minute stop. Five minutes that eliminated any possibility of the day being good.

Today's conversation is friendly. Yet I do notice that framing James's open matter-of-factness is the third-person plural as object of his daily business, of keeping "them" on the other side, of stopping any of "them" who cross.

BY 9:00 A.M. it's hot in the San Pedro Valley. I've come down to touch the metal fence at Naco, the valley's only official border crossing. Welded steel panels rise above dry scraped earth. My car sits next to stacks of massive, rusting steel beams. Elemental building blocks for another wall or for girding this patched fence. I don't know why just then I recall that the remains of a mammoth, impaled by stone points about twelve thousand years ago, were found nearby.

After photographing for a few minutes I step into sight of a Border Patrol truck hidden in the alley between steel stacks and fence line. Its view to the east clear other than dips and swales of small channels. A second patrol vehicle pulls up to me within a minute.

Agent G. Rubsamen is more formal than James. His weapon prominent, he asks why I'm here. Once satisfied he points to the east, "This is the busiest stretch. . . . See that trailer?"

I nod.

"We use horse patrols to catch them, like in that swale where the fence is low."

Voices have sputtered from his radio without pause. Now a louder, more urgent tone. He increases the volume. As if on cue another hidden patrol vehicle accelerates along the fence toward the swale. Its lights flashing.

"They're like monkeys, you know," he adds. We both watch.

I'm ready to leave. No . . . I want him to leave but ask one more question. "What's the fence like across the San Pedro River?"

Agent Rubsamen regards me for a moment before responding. "Oh, there's something there so animals, deer, can get back and forth."

"Something there" I learn are Normandy-style crossed rails in the low floodplain and channel when flow is low, barricades that supposedly can be moved for monsoon floods. Once just barbed wire stretched across the channel, weighted by a large stone. Before that nothing marked where the Mexican San Pedro became American. Now, on either side of the river, thirteen- to eighteen-foot-high fence sections (along with retrofitted gates for flashfloods in small washes) funnel wildlife and people to the channel. There is more surveillance there. Animal movements along the riparian corridor have decreased as helicopters, trucks, and night-lights check more than human migrants.

My fingernail pulls a flake of rust from the border fence of Naco, Arizona. Naco, Sonora, is visible through small gaps between rusted panels.

I suppose it might be easy to be fooled, if one wanted to be, by the legitimacy and seeming once-and-for-allness of this line dividing here from there, "us" from "them." Somewhat permeable at southeastern Arizona's still-open ports of entry: Nogales, Naco, Douglas. Somewhat occluded at the river. Supposedly impermeable where the new fence stands, until you notice repaired cutouts.

Had the outcomes of diplomacy, war, and compromise ended in other ways, the continental United States might look quite different. I stand on homeland of tribal peoples. I stand on land claimed in name by Spain for longer than this country has existed. Nominal possession changed hands to an independent Mexico in 1821 then to the United States three decades later. Control would require a war of conquest and violent dispossessing.

Still cool to the touch this morning, this fence began in an engineered conflict with Mexico—a dispute over territory and borders that many historical accounts present as an inevitable series of events. With my back to the fence I look north, past the western flank of the Mule Mountains, where the mining boomtown of Bisbee sits. North in my mind's eye across mountains, deserts, and plateaus more than ten degrees of latitude to where the imagined northern edge of Nueva España, then Mexico, once lay.

The two-year conflict, a preemptive "war" with Mexico, evoked bitter and intense opposition from start to finish. Its numerous critics believed this war was, in the words of historian John Schroeder, "unnecessary, impolitic, illegal, and immoral." Indeed, even the outbreak of hostilities lay shrouded behind extremely suspicious circumstances. Yet by its end in 1848 Mexico had lost nearly half its claimed territory to the United States. With a "purchase" of more land from Mexico five years later, the United States assumed continental dimensions that would become the "lower forty-eight." This conflict would also serve as the American military's first experience of invading, occupying, and waging extended warfare in another country. The generation of junior officers who cut their teeth then would wage war on each other a decade and a half later.

The noise of arms in battle didn't reach the San Pedro Valley, but the conflict's outcome created this line I turn to face.

*

THE PRESIDENTIAL ELECTION in November 1844 was close. James K. Polk, a Democrat from Tennessee and cotton plantation owner, hadn't won an absolute majority over his Whig opponent, Kentucky Senator Henry Clay. But he took the narrow win as a mandate for aggressive territorial expansion. On his inauguration night in March of 1845, Mr. Polk declared his aim to acquire California from Mexico and to settle the Oregon Territory question with Great Britain. Congress had just approved annexing the Republic of Texas. By the end of March, Mexico would break off diplomatic relations. The southern boundary of Texas, and territory claimed by both nations, lay at the center of increasing rancor. The Nueces River flows some 50 to nearly 150 miles northeast of the Rio Grande, and it had been the Texas border recognized by both governments. The region between the rivers, a land controlled by Mexico and inhabited by citizens of Mexico, was now being claimed by the Republic of Texas.

Even before Texas had accepted annexation to enter the Union as a "slave state," even before exhausting diplomatic channels with Mexico, the president ordered General Zachary Taylor's troops into the republic, then to the Rio Grande, where they aimed cannons across the river at the port town of Matamoros. "General Taylor came into my tent this morning," Colonel Ethan Allen Hitchcock entered in his diary. "I discovered this time more clearly than ever that the General is instigated by ambition—or so it appears to me. He seems quite to have lost all respect for Mexican rights and is willing to be an instrument of Mr. Polk for pushing our boundary as far west as possible." Hitchcock added, "I think the General wants an additional brevet, and would strain a point to get it."

Provoked to do so, Mexican soldiers fired the first shot in April of 1846. Taylor's dispatch to Polk, "Hostilities may now be considered as commenced," arrived in Washington two weeks later, on the evening of May 9th. Earlier that day the president had tried to convince his cabinet that preemptive war was necessary because "the danger was imminent" and there was "ample cause" for action. With the general's news, Mr. Polk asked Congress to recognize that war already existed "notwithstanding all our efforts to avoid it." He argued that "Mexico has passed the boundary of the United States, has invaded our territory and shed American blood upon the American soil." By May 13th the president had his war. Its immediate cause wasn't lost on Colonel Hitchcock: "I have said from the first that the United States are the aggressors. . . . We have not one particle of right to be here. . . . It looks as if the government sent a small force on purpose to bring on a war, so as to have a pretext for taking California and as much of this country as it chooses." As a military man, Hitchcock felt bound to follow orders.

Acrimonious dissent came from many quarters, churning within a cauldron of conflicting biases and agendas between Whigs and Democrats, abolitionists and planters, clergy and laymen. Critics decried Polk's tactics to grab territory by "invasion, conquest, and plunder." Abraham Lincoln, new to the House of Representatives, called for the president to identify exactly where "American" blood had been shed, challenging the literal ground upon which Polk had built his case. Abolitionists and anti-slavery congressmen feared westward expansion of the "peculiar institution," believing war only promoted slaveholders' interests. Frederick Douglass referred to the "disgraceful, cruel, and iniquitous" conflict as a "murderous war—as a war against the free states—as a war against freedom, against the Negro, and against the interests of workingmen of this country—and as a means of extending that great evil and damning curse, negro slavery."

On the other side were those who envisaged new territory making the United States an economic power from coast to coast. Still others said they believed victory would spread American freedom and democracy to more people.

I think the responses of two men bookend opposing sentiments best. One man coined a term in the July-August 1845 issue of the *United States Magazine and Democratic Review*, which he edited. Urging Texas annexation and the country's continued expansion to the Pacific, John L. O'Sullivan called for "the fulfillment of our manifest destiny to overspread the continent allotted by Providence for the free development of our yearly multiplying millions."

The other man denounced the war. After refusing to pay Massachusetts's poll tax in the summer of 1846, he spent a night in the Concord jail. "A common and natural result of an undue respect for law," Henry David Thoreau later wrote in "Civil Disobedience," "is, that you may see a file of soldiers . . . marching in admirable order over hill and dale to the wars, against their wills, ay, against their common sense and consciences, which makes it very steep marching indeed."

But anti-war did not have to mean pro-Mexico or anti-slavery. "Ours is the government of the white man," South Carolina senator John C. Calhoun argued, opposing a proposal to take all of Mexico. "The great misfortune of what was formerly Spanish America, is to be traced to the fatal error of placing the colored race on an equality with the white." Fear of "impure breeds" contaminating Anglo-Saxon blood crossed party line and geography, north to south, Democrat and Whig.

By the terms of the Treaty of Peace, Friendship, Limits, and Settlement signed in the village of Guadalupe Hidalgo on February 2, 1848, Mexico relinquished all claims to Texas. The Rio Grande, not the Nueces River, became the international boundary. Mexico ceded Alta California and Nuevo México. In return the United

States withdrew its forces, canceled Mexico's debts, and paid nearly fifteen million dollars for the ceded territory. Working together, a joint boundary commission was to locate the new two-thousand-mile border. The United States also agreed on paper to guarantee property rights of Mexicans and their descendants now caught north of the line.

The treaty did nothing to resolve the divisive issue of slavery, and attempts to ban the institution in the ceded lands met defeat. Another unresolved tension lay in conflicting interpretations of Article XI: "Considering that a great part of the territories, which, by the present treaty, are to be comprehended for the future within the limits of the United States, is now occupied by savage tribes, who will hereafter be under the exclusive control of the Government of the United States, and whose incursions within the territory of Mexico would be prejudicial in the extreme, it is solemnly agreed that all such incursions shall be forcibly restrained by the Government of the United States." Mexico demanded protection and compensation. Though agreeing to the former, the American government failed to stop raids. It rejected any responsibility for compensation.

The conflict ended as it began. Opponents in Congress had denounced the war while feeling compelled to support the army. Now they denounced a treaty they would ultimately ratify. To the *National Intelligencer*, Washington's Whig newspaper, the sense that "*we take nothing* BY CONQUEST . . . is alone worth far more to a Christian Nation than the sum we shall pay. The lust of Conquest is as unjust and ruinous in a Republic as in any other form of government. . . . Thank God, we shall be saved from the curse of this blighting principle!"

Maps of the United States had to be redrawn yet again, soon after the addition of the Oregon Territory. (In June 1846 Congress had ratified a treaty with Great Britain ending joint occupation; the

United States claimed the Pacific and Rocky Mountains northwest south of the forty-ninth parallel.) Now maps had to include Texas and most of what lay west of the hundredth meridian—what are now the states of California, Nevada, Utah, Arizona, New Mexico, and parts of Colorado, Wyoming, Kansas, and Oklahoma.

MY HAND STILL touches the fence. La Gran Línea. From his parked vehicle Agent Rubsamen can see me in his rearview mirror. Yes, one could be fooled by an illusion of always. But why *here*, why latitude 31°20'N?

Article V of the Treaty of Guadalupe Hidalgo defined the "boundary line between the two Republics" in general terms. Surveyors from both nations on the joint commissions had to locate the precise line that hereafter would "be religiously respected." From the West Coast the border would follow the established line between Baja and Alta California inland to the Colorado River. Its eastern end would begin offshore, in the Gulf of Mexico, from the mouth of the deepest channel of the Rio Grande (or Río Bravo del Norte) and follow the river upstream. Separating "with due precision" the interior tracts of northern Sonora and Chihuahua from the ceded land lying between the two rivers would prove more difficult.

The treaty had delimited the southern boundary of the new American province as that "laid down" on the 1847 map by John Disturnell, *Mapa de los Estados Unidos de Méjico*. But Disturnell was a businessman, not a cartographer. His sources, though not yet officially replaced, still derived from patchy exploratory encounters from the century's first decades. Interior dimensions, edges, and landscape features ranged from approximate to conjecture. Even the U.S. treaty commissioner thought the map "suddenly got up, as the mere speculation of an engraver or bookseller, to meet the demand in our country for Maps of Mexico." Without ground-truthing, the Rio Grande was drawn too far east. Uncertainty over where to put the international boundary west of the river exacerbated tensions between the two nations. At stake within the disputed minutes of latitude were mines and a topographically plausible railroad route that was supported with particular enthusiasm by Southern members of Congress.

By the 1848 treaty terms, Tucson and where I stand still belonged to Mexico. Sonora's northern boundary lay far to the north along the Gila River. Phoenix didn't exist. Nearly six years would pass before the Gadsden "Purchase," or, as it's known in Mexico, El Tratado de la Mesilla, would claim this nether land for the United States.

School history texts still present the purchase as "settling" disputes over placement of the border west of the Rio Grande. The statement is straightforward: For ten million dollars the United States claimed what is now southern New Mexico and Arizona south of the Gila River, nearly thirty thousand square miles. But in trying to smooth and simplify an unsettled, complex story, what's often left out is the smoldering fuse of sectional conflict that would ignite in 1861. Missing from such accounts is that James Gadsden, a South Carolina railroad promoter and plantation owner, had tracks rather than stars in his eyes. Or that Jefferson Davis, then secretary of war, recommended him as minister to Mexico. Gadsden "negotiated" the disputed strip plus enough land farther west for a possible rail corridor to the coast. (*The New York Herald* called it "God-forsaken country"; *The New York Times* dubbed it "a dreary district.") What else is missing is that northern skeptics saw this as a land grab corrupting political process by "South Carolina diplomacy" to link Southern markets with the West Coast. Accounts also tend not to mention that the treaty came to the U.S. Senate in 1854 as it considered the Kansas-Nebraska bill, once again inflaming sectional wounds. The question of where to put the boundary fomented bitter debate. Compromise amendments finally allowed its passage with a compromise latitude. Most accounts, of course, fail to acknowledge Mexican views of the "war of conquest" or either treaty.

Boundary commission teams of surveyors and astronomers, topographers and draftsmen criss-crossed the borderlands between 1849 and 1855. They carried telescopes, transits, theodolites, compasses, barometers, surveying chains, goniometers, chronometers. To locate border coordinates, to fix the meridian and parallel grid onto the land, they aimed their instruments at the moon, sun, and stars. As they made and marked the "true line, from which there shall be no appeal or departure," they also mapped the lay of the land to either side. And by following the plan to "note the general character of the country, in its applicability to agriculture, roads and navigation," the American commission claimed the ceded land more fully. The inland stretch west of the Rio Grande was the last to be surveyed and mapped. No fence cut through it.

Fifty-two monuments—from piled rocks to cut stone and cast iron—marked the boundary on the ground as unconnected dots. Many were destroyed. By the turn of the twentieth century, other joint commissions had resurveyed la línea, repairing old monuments and installing new obelisks. The eventual 276 monuments came closer to connected stitching. Solid divides lay on maps and in minds.

For years a railroad spike driven into the ground marked the border here at Naco, as a community and culture grew together, *ambos*, on both sides. Now that line is embedded.

I stand at a compromise on compromised ground.

The war's outcome set the stage for the next critical piece of the border story that leads to my mother and me. Writing in 1935 the geographer Carl Sauer would note that the "American-Mexican boundary is due more largely to the barrier which the Apache formed from the Gila river to the Texas plains than to any other cause."

. . .

At 7:40 a.m., sunglasses, wide-brimmed hat, and water seem barely adequate to greet the April sun. The trail to the San Pedro River is an exposed shadeless walk one and a half miles into glare. I count my steps to the abandoned railroad grade, trying not to replay the TV interview I'd overheard in the breakfast room of the Desert Rose Inn. From the large-screen TV the governor of Arizona spoke with a Fox News host about the Supreme Court decision on the state's immigration law.

A raven's single caw breaks a breezeless silence. Ahead the San Pedro's riverine green bends through hills and clefts of muted browns. Along the river cottonwood leaves shift in a gentle riparian breath. Vermilion flycatcher, red-winged blackbird, perhaps an Ab-ert's towhee, and a phoebe of some sort are here, too—these are the voices I recognize of many avian conversations. I try to walk into the eighteenth century.

Mounds and rounded mud edges rise above the ground near the river terrace's edge. Creosote and other dryland shrubs partly hide foundation stones and pieces of adobe walls. These are the remains of Presidio de Santa Cruz de Terrenate, a military outpost first gar-risoned in 1776 as one last attempt to control the San Pedro Valley in Nueva España's frontera del norte. It was abandoned four years later.

With a chapel, barracks, family quarters, cannon bastion, and plaza, the presidio at its peak housed perhaps three hundred. The story of its brief life appears on a simple metal cross placed by sol-diers honoring soldiers across two centuries:

Real Presidio de
Santa Cruz de Terrenate
1776–1780

Muerto en Batalla
(KILLED IN ACTION)

7 July 1776
Capt. Francisco Tovar
29 Soldados

24 Sept. 1778
Capt. Francisco Trespalacios
27 Soldados

Nov. 1778 – Feb. 1779
39 Soldados

May 1779
Capt. Luis del Castillo

PLACED BY
WARRANT OFFICERS OF FORT HUACHUCA

The presidio had been designed to withstand sieges, not repeated Apache raids on it and its supply trains. Unable to protect colonists, let alone defend itself, the garrison retreated farther south into Sonora to the San Pedro headwaters after four horrendous years.

But realigning far-flung outposts along la frontera norteña could do little to strengthen a faltering colonial grip. Settlements had taken hold in the Santa Cruz Valley to the west, after the discovery of silver nuggets (*planchas de platas*) not far from present-day Nogales in 1736. Tucson became the largest. But Nueva España's tentative reach into the San Pedro Valley receded southward on an ebbing tide. Hegemony ended at the edge of Apachería. As Juan de

Oñate complained in 1599, the "Apaches . . . are a people that has not yet publicly rendered obedience to his majesty."

AS A CHILD I took large doses of Hollywood westerns. John Ford's were favorites. *She Wore a Yellow Ribbon. Rio Grande. 3 Godfathers.* Of course, Howard Hawks's *Red River.* In clear sharp light accentuated in black-and-white film, landscapes were for me the most vital characters. Owens Valley, Monument Valley, the Colorado River valley between Moab and Cisco, Death Valley, the Mojave Desert, Sedona, Gallup—and, as I now know, this terrain around the Huachuca Mountains.

It was easy to detect geographic fictions. Monument Valley didn't adjoin a Mojave desert playa as *Stagecoach* would have you believe. But cultural fictions were harder for a ten-year-old to fathom.

Oñate may have been among the first to use *Apache*, a word bestowed upon people who conceived of themselves by other terms. Native author and ethnohistorian Jack Forbes points out that names of related tribal peoples—Janos, Jocomes, Sumas—disappeared from Spanish records of this area as the use of *Apache* became prominent. "There seems to be little doubt but that most of them were either absorbed by the Apache or simply came to be called Apaches," Forbes argues. Labels stuck.

In "Apache" eyes, the Spaniards were the aggressors. They had invaded homelands, torn fragile webs of subsistence. Divide-and-rule tactics of the military and Catholic missionaries disrupted alliances and any peaceful relations with the Sobaipuri (O'odham ancestors in the San Pedro Valley). Spanish officials hoped the Sobaipuri and the valley itself could be buffers between *los indios bárbaros* and colonial settlements populated by *gente de razón*. But colonial military campaigns only increased the Apache need for subsistence raids, when their crops or seasonal gathers couldn't be guaranteed.

Escalating warfare of retaliation answered Spanish slave raids, mass murders, rapes, and village destruction.

Two Spanish military men, both astute observers of Nueva España's frontera norteña in the 1790s, offer rare glimpses of the impact of Spanish colonialism on Apache life and livelihood. Lieutenant Colonel Don Antonio Cordero had learned Native languages and knew the names by which the people called themselves. He recognized the seasonality of food gathering and of subsistence raiding in lean times. Observing Chiricahua bands most closely, Lieutenant José María Cortés contended that they desired peace, that those who acted in violence were exceptions, responding in kind to violence directed against them. In his *Memorias sobre las Provincias del Norte de Nueva España* (1799), Cortés noted:

It has been and continues to be our absurd and foolish belief that they are impossible to force into peace and the customs of a rational life, but this is a most patent fallacy. They love peace and hate to lose it. Since the year 1786, when we began to fight them with greater expertise and tactics, we have seen many *rancherías* from different tribes come in to seek peace. It is true that some *rancherías* have struck their encampments and gone to seek refuge in their mountains, but if we examine their reasons in honest truth, we will find that they are justifiable. It is no inconstancy to break the peace when agreements have been breached, for everyone knows that such conduct is employed by the most civilized powers boasting the highest human character.

The "greater expertise and tactics" included eliminating incentives for raids. In exchange for settling rancherías or villages near presidios, Apaches would receive food, cloth, liquor, and "inferior" (that is, easily broken) firearms. The policy's goal: Sabotaging traditional subsistence bases and autonomy would fragment social coherence and defuse the people's will to fight. The alternative to pacified dependence was war. Spanish mines and ranches began to appear in the San Rafael and San Pedro Valleys, and on the Sonoita Plain.

But after 1821, a newly independent Mexico had few funds to subsidize rations. It pursued, instead, a campaign of extermination. Sonoran waterways had already drawn Anglo-American mountain men like James O. Pattie and his father who trapped beaver along the San Pedro River. Other Americans came for Sonora's bounty on Apache scalps: That of an adult man brought one hundred pesos at one point. Scalp hunters determined to make money could kill easier targets with straight black hair. And tales of mineral riches never ceased to entice prospectors to as-yet untapped mountains.

So it doesn't surprise me that prospectors and miners filled half the new Arizona Territorial Legislature when it first convened in 1864. Nor does it surprise that a resolution calling for the extermination of all Apaches was among its first agenda items to be adopted unanimously. The legislature then sought help from the federal government "in subduing our hostile foe" so citizens could "thereby reclaim from the savage one of the most valuable portions of our public domain." In their eyes "nearly every mountain is threaded with veins of gold, silver, copper, and lead."

Settlers came. In 1870 Arizona Territory's Anglo-American population fell just shy of ten thousand. More than forty thousand lived there a decade later. By 1890, four years after Geronimo surrendered two valleys to the east of the San Pedro, their numbers had grown more. By then the U.S. Army had established fifty camps and forts in the territory. What Spain had attempted on its frontera norteña would now be accomplished in the Territory of Arizona.

Vincent Colyer, as secretary to the Board of Indian Commissioners, observed in 1871 that "according to the records of the Indian Department, the Apache Indians were the friends of the Americans when they first knew them." Yet the army's frontier defense in and around the San Pedro Valley took offensive form reminiscent of the Spanish military. Beyond direct attacks, detachments burned rancherías, destroying crops and other resources to force Apache into dependence on rations. "Savage, treacherous and cruel as these Indians are," one officer noted in 1871, "they still have enough of human nature in their composition to consider them controllable through the medium of their bellies." U.S. Army records and territorial newspapers of the time show that the number of Apaches killed in southern Arizona was many times that of Anglo casualties.

Violence and fear were marketable, and Arizona Territory's economy grew to depend on supply contracts with the army. Numerous businessmen found it profitable to be at war with the Apache—that is, until more lucrative mining ventures pushed for an end to hostilities.

TWO ARMY POSTS in the San Pedro Valley helped define the so-called Apache wars: Camp Grant near the river's mouth and Fort Huachuca near Mexico. Both posts would also play huge roles in delimiting borders and terms of migration for years to come. My mother hasn't yet arrived on the scene but a chain of events associated with both places anticipates her presence and that of other African Americans. The consequences still unfold; they are still palpable. My presence in the San Pedro Valley and these words form but another link.

My visit to the Presidio de Santa Cruz de Terrenate began a long day of downstream wandering to the San Pedro River's mouth, more than ninety miles to the north. A day of motion through heat and time, from the ruins of an eighteenth-century military outpost to the site of a nineteenth-century army camp. The same river and, in many ways, the same frontier. Heat broke at last as large cumulus clouds crowned the Santa Catalina and Galiuro ranges rimming the valley. They'd framed my view for hours. Winds soon buffeted my car. Rain fell when I crossed Aravaipa Creek. Camp Grant once sat where the creek empties into the San Pedro, a few miles south of its junction with the Gila River. For the Tcéjìné (Dark Rocks People, or Aravaipa band of the Ndee) and 'Tìs'évàn (Cottonwoods in Gray Wedge Shape People or Pinal band) this place was core to their traditional homelands. They called the stream's confluence Łednłíí (Flows Together).

Members of several bands sought peace at Camp Grant in early 1871. The hard winter left little food, with crops and stores destroyed by the army. The Ndee moved upstream on Aravaipa Creek and received rations of flour, sugar, coffee, corn, meat, and calico cloth.

Blood had spilled at Aravaipa Creek many times over the preceding century. The last attack would occur in the still-dark morning of April 30, 1871, when a vigilante group of white and Mexican Tucson residents with Tohono O'odham allies massacred more than one hundred, nearly all sleeping women and children, at Gashdla'á Cho O'áá (Big Sycamore Stands There). The attackers took perhaps thirty children captive, most of them likely sold into slavery.

In the ensuing trial, a jury of peers deliberated less than twenty minutes before acquitting all defendants. The reputations of many like William Oury, one of the vigilante leaders, seemed enhanced by the perceived courage and rightness of their actions. The massacre also helped crystallize President Grant's peace policy, an attempt at a feasible guide for the Department of the Interior's Indian Bureau, a guide supporting reservation confinement and conversion to civilized Christianity. As representative of the Board of Indian Commissioners and the Peace Commission, Vincent Colyer toured southeastern Arizona months after the massacre. A Quaker derisively called "Vincent the Good," Colyer tried to persuade Apache groups to settle in reserved tracts within their homelands yet "remote from white settlement." For the Tcéjìné and 'Tìs'évàn who wished to stay, he established a reserve around Aravaipa Creek and the downstream reaches of the San Pedro River. He also visited Gashdla'á Cho O'áá along Aravaipa Creek and saw that "skulls of the Indians, with the temple-bones beaten in, lay exposed by the washing of the run and the feeding of the wolves."

Colyer's efforts enraged Arizona citizens and more than a few army officers. "A rascal who comes here to thwart the attempts of military and citizens to conquer a peace from our savage foe, deserves to be stoned to death," ran one *Arizona Miner* editorial. The secretary of the interior then directed Major General Oliver Otis Howard to Arizona and New Mexico early in 1872 "for the purpose of preserving peace." The secretary harbored a remote hope that, beyond settling the Apaches on reservations, Howard might persuade Anglo settlers "to treat the Indians with humanity, justice, and forbearance." This namesake of Howard University, and commissioner of the Freedmen's Bureau, held a "peace conference" at Camp Grant a year after the massacre. It brought together representatives of most sides and corners involved: Tucson citizens, Tohono O'odham and Akimel O'odham leaders, army officers, the territorial governor, federal bureaucrats, and grieving Apache. The *Arizona Weekly Citizen* reported on May 25, 1872, that Santo (or Santos), a leader of the Aravaipa band, began the proceedings: "Arizing and going before the General and laying a small stone on the floor, he said that he did not know how to read or write, this is his paper (pointing to the stone), and he wants a peace that will last as long as that stone lasts."

By the conference's terms the Aravaipa and Pinal bands were to move north to a reservation along the San Carlos and Gila Rivers, though some would try to remain in the San Pedro watershed until forced out. General Howard then negotiated a tentative peace with Cochise, leader of the Chiricahua Apaches, in their Dragoon Mountains "stronghold" nearer the border with Mexico. The promised reservation was to embrace homeland in the Chiricahua, Dragoon, and Mule Mountains east of the San Pedro Valley. But within four years the president would revoke the executive order reserving the land. Then silver was struck in the nearby Tombstone Hills, and copper discoveries sparked Bisbee's boom in what had been Chiricahua land. And the War Department, skeptical of Grant's peace policy from the first, would in the end abide by General Crook's belief that only absolute defeat could convince "renegade" Apaches to retire to reservations.

William Tecumseh Sherman, then commanding general of the U.S. Army, thought the reservations "seem far enough removed from the white settlements to avoid the dangers of collision of interest." He was wrong. Collisions of interest would continue stepwise dispossessings well into the twentieth century. Forced to migrate to a reservation where they'd be confined with other tribal groups, Western Apache bands left their San Pedro homeland and life base. Then the reserved land itself was whittled away.

For even as the San Carlos Reservation was being created, prospectors discovered silver and copper in its western reaches near present-day Globe. They found copper to the east. Dismantling the promised reservation began with a string of executive orders that, slice by slice, "restored to public domain" pieces of reserved land found valuable. North America's largest copper producer for years, the Morenci mine, lies on former reserved land. The state's Coolidge Dam on the Gila River flooded the best farmland of the reservation in the 1920s to help create, with other dams and diversions on this river and its tributaries like the Salt, an "agricultural empire" downstream. Phoenix rose not from ashes but from irrigated acres.

I visited the San Carlos Apache Cultural Center in Peridot on Highway 70 after leaving Aravaipa Creek. No longer the rhythmic basin, range, basin, range, the terrain had become an upland of range after range—Dripping Springs, Mescal, Pinal—incised by steep canyons and set apart by broad, dry tablelands. I'd come to meet and thank Mr. Herb Stevens, who'd generously given his time when I told him of my search. He spoke of memories of family returning to the Huachuca Mountains, and the fort, to gather acorns from Emory oaks. The cultural center's museum displays Ndeh experiences past to present, the "tragedy" at Camp Grant, and the people's survival as part of the origin of the San Carlos Apache. The center's website states that the reservation "is the world's first concentration camp still existing to this day."

WHAT MIGHT BE called "official" history positioned the massacre near Camp Grant as part of inevitable collisions between civilization and savagery from which the West was won. This unambiguous story justified violence. Participants in the massacre, many of them notable Tucson citizens, founded the Society of Arizona Pioneers in 1884. I learned, too, that some of the first materials of this precursor to the Arizona Historical Society were produced to explain why righteous ends justified drastic means. Later writers would use these documents, Tucson newspaper accounts, and army reports as the basis of history.

The events of that April dawn in 1871 and their meanings now have come under a brighter light. Three remarkable books published within a year and a half of each other—*Massacre at Camp Grant* (by Chip Colwell-Chanthaphonh), *Shadows at Dawn* (by Karl Jacoby), and *Big Sycamore Stands Alone* (by Ian Record)—recognize other forms of remembrance, other conceptions of time, space, and life in these borderlands. Mexican corridos, Tohono O'odham calendar sticks, Ndeh oral histories and traditions stand alongside those documents long privileged in scholarship. The three books show how the massacre, and mindsets behind it, both destroyed and created history. "Violence may begin as a contest over resources," Karl Jacoby writes, "but it often ends as contest over meaning." And, so, perpetrators tried to ensure that their actions and reasons for acting had prominent and positive places in historical accounts. Silenced from public history were not only those killed; muted, too, were the voices of survivors.

Violence created physical and conceptual border(ed)lands—reservations and bounded narratives. Removal, forced migration, and containment seemed necessary for both. They also defined the San Pedro space African Americans would enter.

• • •

"If any one post of the United States Army might lay claim to being home station for the Buffalo Soldiers, that post would be Fort Huachuca. Both all-black cavalry regiments served there, both all-black infantry regiments, and, during World War II, both all-black infantry divisions." So Cornelius C. Smith Jr. begins chapter 18 of his history of this "frontier post." And in two sentences my mother and her service become linked to Apache "wars," to an unpatrolled international border, and to a Jim Crow army that tolerated and preferred to use "colored" soldiers in remote outposts. Military custom and events of the nineteenth century forged another link to the chain that drew her to the edge of the San Pedro Valley by Mexico. She would experience, in the 1940s, borders and migrations of a different sort.

The African American presence in Arizona and at Fort Huachuca began with the "Indian wars" and with a bitter debate in Congress at the close of the Civil War. Should Black men be allowed to serve in a peacetime army? Their proven record in segregated Union units in the recent conflict eventually made compromise possible. Sixty regiments of the Regular Army would include a few "all Negro" units: the 9th Cavalry and 10th Cavalry regiments (the latter the first to be called "Buffalo Soldiers"), and four foot units that were consolidated in 1869 as the 24th and 25th infantry regiments. White officers, of course, would command every "all Negro" unit.

Army assignments tended to rotate between the frontier and more populated areas to the east. At least this was the case for white units. African American regiments more often than not remained on western posts until the Spanish-American War in 1898—and after serving abroad many were returned to the West. The War Department's reasoning: The presence of armed Black men in uniform in densely settled eastern states and, particularly, in the South could only lead to racial violence. Better to confine them to remote areas. Such belief-driven policies would guide War Department decisions about African Americans in the military through the Second World War.

Fort Huachuca was the last of the network of army garrisons set up south of the Gila River before Geronimo's surrender in 1886. The rest, like Camp Grant, were abandoned or deactivated. Many lie in ruins. The fort is now home to the U.S. Army Intelligence Center. It also boasts the world's largest unmanned aircraft systems training center. Drones fly there.

The post began in March of 1877 as Camp Huachuca, the same year silver was found across the valley in the Tombstone Hills. Situated where a wooded glen with a perennial stream opens onto the northeastern flank of the Huachuca Mountains, the site offers a spectacular vantage of the San Pedro basin and nearby ranges. One stated purpose of the camp was to protect the ever-growing numbers of settlers as well as travel routes near the international border. One military historian put it in more blunt terms: A primary goal was to reduce if not eliminate "Apache depredations" along "plunder trails" into Sonora. The temporary camp became Fort Huachuca early in 1882—months after the shootout at the OK Corral—as booms of silver in Tombstone and copper in Bisbee lured thousands of fortune seekers and settlers.

Although not stationed at Fort Huachuca at the time, African American troops of the 10th Cavalry served in the army's campaign against Geronimo, crossing the border between Sonora and Arizona Territory in chase. When companies of the 24th Infantry arrived at the fort in 1892, this post overlooking the San Pedro Valley became the destination of migrations of "Negro" soldiers by military order. All four African American regiments had called the fort home by the early 1930s. Their primary duty after the "Apache wars" was to patrol a fenceless international border. This included the decade of revolutions in Mexico. Where I stood at Naco, "neutral" troops of the 10th and 9th cavalry units placed flags to mark the border during a fight between rival Mexican factions in 1914. It was an ironic attempt to keep fire south of the line while American arms shipments crossed it to support the Carranzistas. The 10th Cavalry entered Mexico in 1916—along with airplanes in their first military use—on General Pershing's Punitive Expedition after Pancho Villa. Border tensions quickly escalated after Germany offered an alliance to help Mexico reclaim its lost northern territory, should the United States enter the First World War.

The most massive migration in uniform would come when Fort Huachuca became the training station for the 93rd and 92nd infantry divisions, the only "all-Negro" divisions in the Second World War. Nineteenth-century policies remained the rule: White officers would command otherwise segregated units. "Leadership is not imbedded in the Negro race yet"—this diary entry by Secretary of War Henry Stimson in 1940 expressed the underlying sense of military staff. The draft still prohibited mingling of "colored and white" in the same army units. "WHITE HOUSE BLESSES JIM CROW" ran one newspaper headline.

Jim Crow remained official policy and unofficial custom. African American troops would train, serve, and live in separate facilities, and the War Department's rationale for choosing Fort Huachuca followed old reasoning. The isolated post had hosted Black soldiers for more than half a century. The few settlements in and around the San Pedro Valley at least had some experience with "colored men." The post could also be expanded down the mountain's alluvial slope toward the San Pedro River if need be.

So Fort Huachuca quickly became two posts in one. Facilities were duplicated with a segregated new cantonment area built down-slope of the original site. Like a fast-forwarded cartoon, more than a thousand new buildings sprang up. Eventually there were duplicate sets of barracks and civilian quarters. Two officers' clubs. Two station hospitals. Two sets of chapels, theaters, service clubs, day rooms—even flagpoles.

Thousands of African American men converged at Fort Huachuca under orders as they had over the years, but on an unprecedented scale. This time, too, African American women migrated in uniform, as army nurses like my mother and as members of the Women's Army Auxiliary Corps (WAAC), later the Women's Army Corps (WAC).

Fort Huachuca became the third largest city in Arizona, after Phoenix and Tucson. Its population exceeded forty-two thousand by 1944, and the 93rd Division's newspaper had the second largest circulation in the state.

But this segregated city resembled no other in the nation.

The fort became a place of many firsts. It was the first post to house and train division-sized units of African American soldiers, their largest concentration ever in one place. It housed the first army station hospital—and regional hospital for a while—to be staffed and commanded by African Americans, with the Medical Corps' first black colonel at the top. That is, at least on paper. With nearly a thousand beds, the hospital was the largest African

American medical facility in the nation at the time, and the first army hospital to give formal basic training to Black nurses. Fort Huachuca was also the first installation to have Black WAACs commanded by Black officers.

Noteworthy firsts such as these might elicit great praise until one realizes they resulted from the military's policies of segregation magnified.

Consensus among the War Department's top brass maintained that Southern white officers understood African American men and possessed the best qualifications to lead them. Ranking officers at Fort Huachuca, from captains to generals, hailed from states like Mississippi, Texas, the Carolinas, Virginia. Major General Edward Almond, commander of the 92nd Division (and former assistant commander of the 93rd), believed Southern officers at Fort Huachuca "understood the characteristic of the Negro and his habits and inclinations" as well as his "capabilities." Almond had a habit of referring to his troops as "nigras." His wife requested separate white and "colored" shopping days on the post. And a commanding officer's response of "I hate niggers" to a Black officer reporting for duty wasn't far out of the ordinary.

"Negro" officers outside of the medical corps and chaplains were frozen in the lowest ranks, rarely rising above first lieutenant. This avoided the inconceivable situation of a Black man commanding a white man. General Almond's "inefficient officer school," his remedial program for those not up to snuff, contained only African Americans. Men in it were college graduates who spoke their minds. Although by far most officers were white, many not as well educated, not one was deemed "inefficient."

Regardless of achievement or position in civilian life, whether from communities in the Northeast or West where at least a hard-won level of integration existed, Black men and women who migrated under orders to Fort Huachuca were thrust into a separate-and-unequal landscape. For those soldiers, nurses, doctors, and service personnel who came from the South, their posting verified that segregated America extended far beyond home. None could easily leave.

Fry, Sierra Vista's predecessor, was the civilian town at the mountain base. Shanties, shacks, and trailers spread out along the post's eastern fence like blown tumbleweeds. Fry's chief stocks in trade, as one officer put it, were bootleg alcohol, juke joints, "prostitutes in their waning years of professional endeavor," and venereal disease. The next closest point on the map was Hereford, a whistle-stop on the San Pedro River by the border. Its rail station had latrines out back labeled "colored" and "colored women." Wartime gasoline and rubber restrictions isolated the post further from distant communities. Those who could reach Bisbee or Nogales, Tucson or Phoenix risked unwanted encounters with civilian police, white soldiers, and MPs.

"We must be self-contained as possible in all recreational, cultural, and entertainment activities," post commander Colonel Edwin Hardy explained to an *Arizona Daily Star* reporter. Black women at the post, in particular the WAACs, learned that their presence was partly meant as incentive to keep Black men from entering relationships with white and Mexican women. Self-containment aimed to ensure the color line would remain sharp and uncrossed.

The civilian atmosphere added further insult to injury, as in the fall of 1942 when Arizona governor Sidney Osborn sought the army's help in filling a labor shortage for the cotton harvest. The Associated Press reported the governor as saying, "I am sure there are many thousands of experienced cotton pickers at Huachuca and I am sure that they could be put at nothing more necessary, essential or vital at this particular moment than aiding in the harvesting of this crop."

*

I'VE SPENT SEVERAL days at the National Archives II in College Park, Maryland, searching through army records and files of the civilian aide to the secretary of war for references to Fort Huachuca and the military's policy regarding race and medical facilities. The minutes of a meeting nine months to the day before Pearl Harbor's bombing set the tone of all I would find. African American leaders in health fields had tried to persuade Surgeon General James C. Magee to reconsider the army's plan to use few Black medical personnel and to establish segregated hospitals and wards. "In a great many northern cities, Negroes are caring for white patients," offered Mrs. Mabel Staupers, executive secretary of the National Association of Colored Graduate Nurses (NACGN). "They are working together in the hospitals." The army's plan would be a huge step backward, they argued, from the great strides made in the North and West where many hospitals and patients accepted "integrated" staff. "These lines have been drawn a long time," Magee countered, "before you and I were born—the problem exists and I don't consider it at all practicable to try to change it. I am quite sure it would be a bad move to so intermingle races."

The meeting minutes, declassified two decades later, suggest many tension-filled moments when dropped pins could be heard by all present. The War Department later put a positive public spin on its policy of segregation. "For the first time in the history of the Army," Undersecretary of War Robert Patterson declared, "opportunity has been furnished the Negro medical profession to exercise full professional talent through the establishment of separate departments at two of our large cantonment hospitals for the care of Negro soldiers."

African American nurses could find no room in the military before 1941. Those applying to the Army Nurse Corps received one response: "Your application for appointment . . . cannot be given favorable consideration as there are no provisions in Army regulations for the appointment of colored nurses in the Corps." The army began to yield, inch by inch, to public pressure brought to bear by Mabel Staupers and the NACGN, raising its quotas for Black nurses by small increments each year of the war. Yet even with a desperate shortage of nurses at home and overseas, the army contemplated (with the president's support) drafting white nurses while excluding large numbers of African American nurses eager to volunteer. Those already in the service were often underutilized. Each patient in Fort Huachuca's Station Hospital Number One, the "colored" hospital, could at one point almost have a dedicated nurse.

"We fail to understand how America can say to the World that in this country we are ready to defend democracy," Staupers wrote to the head of the American Red Cross Nursing Service, "when its Army and Navy is committed to a policy of discrimination." She presented the case to Eleanor Roosevelt in November 1944. Staupers also described to the First Lady the growing pattern of using Black nurses at prisoner-of-war camp hospitals. Was this to be their role in the war, she asked, prisoners the only white men they can care for? "When our women hear of the great need for nurses in the Army and when they enter the Service it is with the high hopes that they will be used to nurse sick and wounded soldiers who are fighting our country's enemies and not primarily to care for these enemies." Mrs. Roosevelt then contacted the secretary of war and surgeon general.

There was no public outcry when the War Department ended segregation and quotas in the Army Nurse Corps on January 20, 1945. By war's end, though, only five hundred or so African American women would be among the fifty thousand nurses in its ranks.

Enter my mother, Vivian Victoria Reeves, a second lieutenant in her early twenties who could join the Army Nurse Corps because of

Mabel Staupers's challenges to the status quo. She was posted at Station Hospital Number One in July 1944, assigned to general duty. The command staff had distinguished records—a who's who in the African American medical profession. The first "Negro" to graduate from Cornell's medical school, the first "Negro" admitted to the American Board of Surgery, the first "Negro" certified by the American Board of Radiology. Lieutenant Colonel M. O. Bousfield, of the Julius Rosenwald Fund, commanded. Few hospitals in the nation could boast such a highly competent and distinguished staff.

Station Hospital Number Two, the "white" hospital, had one-fifth the beds. With the exception of the post surgeon and a few specialists, most of its staff were also African American. An inspector from the army's Medical Corps reported late in the war that "most of the white personnel seek the superior administrations of the colored professional staff at out-patient clinics" of "the excellently organized and maintained Station Hospital No. 1." He also observed that the insistence of "the present Post Surgeon and allegedly some members of the post overhead (white)" on needing a white hospital "reflects the undercurrent of discrimination and antagonism on the post."

*

FORT HUACHUCA
A ~~GOOD~~ PLACE TO REENLIST SINCE 1877
GREAT

Painted words on the water tower greet those entering the post.

Two maps lie unfolded on my passenger seat. The armed sergeant at the main gate gave me one of the current reservation after checking my identification. The other is a hand-drawn diagrammatic plan of the "new cantonment" from about 1943. Detail from the older drawing fills large open patches on the recent map. Without this older plan, a visitor driving up the alluvial fields could miss the relict streets. Grass and scrub have reclaimed much of this land, erupting through and covering broken pavement. Little beyond foundations and cobble walls remains of Station Hospital Number One, or of barracks, PXs, recreational buildings, mess halls, or a chapel. What was once the segregated cantonment is mostly abandoned earth. Signs marking former streets—H2 Rd, H1 Rd, H5 Rd—place the old hospital grounds. Steps lead up to ghosts of buildings. A solitary boarded-up structure stands closer to the mountain front. This is the old Mountain View or "Colored" Officers' Club.

My first visit to Fort Huachuca was years ago. Without any map or guide then, without realizing the hospital no longer stood, I found the old grounds only by luck. This time I have photographs— old snapshots and Kodachrome slides from my mother's things, plus an aerial shot. These images show what's no longer here. A long elevated breezeway. My mother in nurse's whites and in dress uniform—with fellow nurses, alone, with soldiers. The photos also show the alluvial fan's contours and distinctive Huachuca peaks, which guide me to where a twenty-three-year-old Vivian Reeves navigated her way in a Jim Crow army.

Momma's commanding officer at Station Hospital Number One complained repeatedly to the civilian aide to the secretary of war about discriminatory practices against physicians and nurses. These records, too, are now declassified in the National Archives II. Early in autumn of 1944 he wrote of the "very definite trend toward using colored nurses in the Prisoner of War camps" as "again an example of using Negro personnel in places where white nurses object to working." Many of these nurses were reassigned from Fort Huachuca. Mother was transferred to the camp at Florence, Arizona.

*

THIRTY MILES SOUTH of Apache Junction on State Route 79, and about forty river-miles downstream of the San Pedro's mouth, I cross the broad, dry bed of the Gila River. Were this 1849 or 1853, I'd be crossing into Mexico. Today it is WELCOME TO FLORENCE! ELEV. 1493. FOUNDED 1866. Legend has it that as Pinal County's seat the town had a choice in 1908: to host a university or a prison. I was told that it chose the latter. I pass the Arizona State Prison Complex east of the highway.

Buildings of nearly every architectural style from territorial days can be seen along Florence's streets. They feed a sense that the past tags closely along with the present. Time does stand still, too, on the courthouse clock tower overlooking the town. Its metal facings show the correct time twice a day—two minutes to nine or sixteen minutes to noon depending on your reading of the hands—a fixed reminder that building funds ran out in 1891 before clocks could be purchased.

The largest of Arizona's prisoner-of-war camps stood in the Four Parks area just across the Gila River from town on Route 79. The Florence camp first held captured Italians, then German foot soldiers and men from the air corps and panzer divisions. They were shipped from North Africa, France, Belgium, and Italy. Many would end up picking cotton.

Although War Department officials wanted no "social experiments" in the army, African American nurses and German-born Jewish doctors cared for Nazi prisoners at the Florence camp hospital. My mother arrived in March 1945, where she was posted to supervise the operating room. She taught and guided enlisted personnel and prisoners in OR techniques. She scrubbed for major operations and acted as surgeon's assistant. When off duty, though, she and other Black officers couldn't patronize stores, cafes, or other businesses that welcomed and served German prisoners. Whether in Florence or Phoenix it was often the same greeting: "We do not cater to colored." Shortly before she died my mother responded to some of my questions with facts and dates as she could remember: the what, where, and when. She offered no words on how she felt.

Nurses posted at such camps protested to the civilian aide, to the NAACP, to newspapers, and to Mabel Staupers of the NACGN. From the indignities described in letters, Staupers gathered that a problem larger than civilian prejudice "was the prejudice exhibited in camps by white American officers to the Negro nurses who were officers, too, much of it shown in the presence of the prisoners." She described how "prisoners expressed to the nurses their surprise that Americans would fight to preserve democracy abroad and at home exhibit prejudice to other Americans solely because of their skin color." Former prisoners recalled being told by white American officers that white men should not mix with Blacks or Mexicans. The many letters I read in the National Archives present case after case of Nazi prisoners of war having rights and liberties denied to Negro citizen-soldiers. One anonymous letter was written by a nurse contemplating suicide "at a desert post."

After VE Day my mother returned to Fort Huachuca as nursing supervisor for the general ward in Station Hospital Number One. Promoted to first lieutenant and surgical supervisor, she stayed until her discharge in December 1945.

Most of the Florence camp buildings are gone, either demolished or hauled away for other uses. Retirement communities now sit there, along with an Arizona Army National Guard center and a "Service Processing Center" for U.S. Immigration and Customs Enforcement. One of the old hospital buildings is an annex in Caliente Casa de Sol's senior RV park.

An exhibit on the prisoner-of-war camp at McFarland State Historic Park Visitor Center in town gives no word on African

Americans. Just down the street the Pinal County Historical Museum has archived photographs of army personnel at the camp, and Black nurses stand silently there. These images aren't on display with the Tom Mix memorabilia, cactus furniture, hanging nooses used at the state prison, and the chair used for the first gas chamber execution in Arizona.

The public story of African Americans presented at Fort Huachuca's post museum praises the Buffalo Soldiers for their gallantry and self-sacrifice, their rise above prejudice and "quiet dignity lacking outright protest." The story is quick to add that barriers of discrimination "fell faster in the Army" than in "other parts of American society." The World War II stories are of proud firsts and numbers and displayed descriptions like this by Corporal Ernestine Hughes:

> Fort Huachuca on a moonlight night is like a cluster of gems set in a diadem of black velvet. . . . Soldiers and WACs are dancing to the mellow strains of the Post's famous orchestras; others are bowling, skating, seeing movies, or settled down to games of cards, or parked on the desert's edge, romancing under the Huachuca moon.

The museum stories give no hint of what I found in the National Archives. Nothing of the protests against incident after incident, against untried murders, against discriminatory practices. Nothing of the complaints, charges, and calls to justice. Nothing of the case of a young medical officer at Fort Huachuca who was court-martialed and convicted of "behaving with disrespect toward a superior officer" after that ranking officer had yelled "Nigger, stop that damn car!" Confidential records now declassified give clear evidence of the reasons behind low morale and unrest at the then third-largest city in Arizona.

I'll never know what my mother experienced at Fort Huachuca or Florence. I'm also well aware that the charge of catastrophizing could be made at my calling attention to only troubling things. That if averaged over years or over all African American experience in a segregated military, things weren't all that bad. The Huachuca moon surely was there. Yet these long-stored accounts speak to what hasn't been acknowledged in public. Viewed side by side with War Department reports, the sheer volume of once confidential records show some of the lies in the army's slippery bureaucratic language, even as it was becoming a basis for official history. The noncommittal spin of acceptance of one million African Americans into a Jim Crow military, of equal opportunity for "Negro" doctors and nurses within a just and fair segregation that federal officials claimed was "at the request of representatives of the Negro medical profession." The fight for a Double V for victory against fascism overseas and against racism at home wasn't won on at least one front.

BEFORE LEAVING FORT Huachuca I walked around the large wood-framed structure standing alone on the western edge of the segregated cantonment area. Building 66050. Now boarded up, it opened for business on Labor Day in 1942 as the Mountain View or "Colored" Officers' Club.

African American officers boycotted the segregated club at first, refusing to step across its threshold. They wanted the Lakeside Officers' Club, with its guest quarters and other amenities, to admit all officers on the post. Some called Building 66050 "Uncle Tom's Cabin." But most did come to use the Mountain View Club at last.

The historic core of Fort Huachuca, the "old post" high on the mountain fan, became a National Historic Landmark in 1976.

Building 66050 became eligible for the National Register of Historic Places in 1998. As the only existing military service club built specifically for African American personnel, its eligibility is based on its being "associated with events that have made a significant contribution to the broad patterns of our history."

To keep or dismantle what was once unwanted by so many? A segregated club that at first outraged many Black officers has champions today in the NAACP, the Southwest Association of Buffalo Soldiers, and the Tucson Historical Preservation Foundation. Building 66050 found a place on the Arizona Register of Historic Places in 2012 even though the army's historic preservation officers argued its ineligibility for national preservation. It was meant to be a temporary structure, they say. There's no real historical merit. Besides, they add, the elderly men of the Southwest Association of Buffalo Soldiers who were given access to the structure by the army altered its integrity.

The army wants Building 66050 torn down. The National Trust for Historic Preservation listed it as one of the America's 11 Most Endangered Historic Places in June 2013.

Fort Huachuca, Home of the Buffalo Soldier.

• • •

Arizona entered the Union on Valentine's Day in 1912, following New Mexico by a month to become the last of the contiguous forty-eight states. A hundred years later its centennial and historical advisory commissions hoped commemorating this birthday would provide, in their words, "the opportunity to learn from our past and tell all the stories of Arizona that should be told so we continue to move forward with better understanding and empathy among our citizens."

The centennial was meant to be about "the people we are and the people we want to be." The official website, the most public and widest-reaching venue for the year, celebrated the Arizona that "epitomized the economic promise of the American West." This was the "home of the Five C's—copper, cattle, cotton, citrus, and climate." This Arizona supposedly had mined more copper than all other states combined. This Arizona "was founded on rugged individualism matched with hard work and vision."

When all of the website's pages and links were active, I saw a familiar cast of characters prominent in a celebratory story, an Arizona seen through their eyes. The "influences of the state's Native American and Hispanic cultures" alluded to seemed to disappear in layers of stories, fun facts, timelines, and "This Day in Arizona History." "Becoming Arizona," a year-long exhibition at the university in Tucson, featured "maps, books, photographs, letters, scrapbooks and unique items" from its special collections and the Arizona Historical Society. On display were an original print of the 1848 Tratado de Paz (Treaty of Guadalupe Hidalgo), a scrapbook by the first governor, Wyatt Earp's wedding ring, Geronimo's tinder bag, and "William Oury's hand-written speech that seeks to defend his role in the killing of Apache women and children at the Camp Grant massacre of 1871."

The centennial's official book, *Arizona: 100 Years Grand*, focuses on the "long road under many flags" leading to statehood and the years since 1912. I looked for "the people" on each page. Beyond a spread given to Cochise, most references to the Apaches I read are three- or four-word asides: "troubles with the Apaches," "when Apaches attacked," "an Apache attack," "ambushed by Apaches." A single page of text contains African American history, another presents the Tohono O'odham, and another offers words on César Chávez. A page on the internment of Japanese Americans during the Second World War devotes most space to two baseball games played sixty-one years apart—a heartwarming story.

Phantom histories inhabit the spaces between the book's pages, human experiences that still don't fit neatly within official stories or popular habits of mind.

The San Pedro Valley has been contested for centuries. The Mexican War and Gadsden treaty couldn't claim or create a tabula rasa here. Not with tribal peoples indigenous to these basins and ranges. Not as so many *other* peoples came. Mexican citizens, then "immigrants." Chinese immigrants who labored in mines and laid tracks but couldn't live in sundown towns like Bisbee. And those of African heritage, from as early as the 1530s when a man named Esteban or Estevan de Dorantes, survivor of the disastrous Narváez expedition in Florida, may have passed this way. Africans certainly trudged north on Coronado's *entrada*, for it was reported that "negros y indios" died of thirst and hunger. People of mixed African Indigenous, African Mexican, and African European ancestry arrived and stayed. William "Curly" Neal built the famous Mountain View Hotel, a resort in Oracle frequented by Buffalo Bill Cody and other celebrity guests. Jazz legend Charles Mingus, son of an African American soldier and a Mexican woman, was born in Nogales. Black homesteaders settled along the San Pedro River.

I had hoped for even a hint of their voices in the centennial's telling of "all the stories that should be told." I'd hoped for some acknowledgment of mosaics linking cultures, of border crossings, of these places as landscapes of restriction.

So many dividing lines have criss-crossed this valley, seen and unseen, porous and seemingly solid. Visitors to the BLM wilderness area in Aravaipa Canyon can believe they're hiking in pristine nature—one measure of biodiversity valued at a high premium—yet know nothing of the watershed's tragic unnatural history and burden of violence. The metal barrier at Naco marks 31°20'N but gives no hint of the border's one-way permeability. Over a century ago, an American entrepreneur and self-invented "colonel" owned copper mines at the San Pedro's headwaters in Cananea, Sonora. A strike there in 1906 helped kindle the Mexican Revolution. Today, Cananea hosts one of the largest open-pit copper mines in the world, owned and operated by a corporation in which American interests are key.

BEAVER ONCE WERE a keystone species in the San Pedro River, before being trapped and forced out a century ago. Their dams slowed flow enough so water could infiltrate and recharge the aquifer now being tapped out by Fort Huachuca and Sierra Vista. Reintroduced over a decade ago in the riparian conservation area, beavers have migrated downstream to Aravaipa Creek and upstream into Mexico. Would anyone think of them as illegal immigrants?

To *migrate*. To change one's position or residence, to move from one place to another. To pass into a new form or condition, to shift.

"Why do you want to go there?" I couldn't answer my mother's question when she was alive. I'd like to try again. I first came for some clue to her quietness about the past, to her determined dignity. But my reasons soon became much more far-reaching. Frontiers of conquest collided where a small river waters a dry land. The consequences still unfold, reaching past my mother to me.

Gloria Anzaldua called a borderland "a vague and undetermined place created by the emotional residue of the unnatural boundary. It is in a constant state of transition. The prohibited and forbidden are its inhabitants." I write as an outsider to the San Pedro borderlands; my people haven't lived here for generations or called it homeland. Yet here I've crossed many lines and edges—of time, place, and person. Elusive and illusive.

I hold a photograph of my mother. She sits in dress uniform on a step in bright slant light. It could be Fort Huachuca or Florence, 1944 or 1945. Younger than I ever knew her, far younger than I am now, she smiles. Her face turned toward the camera and sun, shapely legs crossed, Vivian Reeves is fully alive in the shutter-clicked moment. She is there; she was there. Absence felt in a change of tense. Touching this image I try to imagine innumerable present moments in this borderland. An afternoon like this day, but in 1542. In April 1871. April 1945. Tomorrow.

PLACING WASHINGTON, D.C., AFTER THE INAUGURATION

I stand in the place my father's kin called home. Ancestors came because this river flows to an ocean across whose waters empires expanded and peoples migrated by choice and force. They came here, too, because of a president's wish for a new capital.

On every visit to Washington, D.C., I come to this river, the Potomac. From where I stay in Glover Park a path follows Foundry Branch through woods of sycamore and beech, tulip poplar and oak, to its mouth. I often walk this forested corridor within the city, at last passing through a dripping, rock-walled tunnel under the C & O Canal to reach the river's edge. Others know this spot, too. Some live here in warm weather, their makeshift shelters under shading canopy. The moments when no one else is about I take as gifts and linger.

The Potomac's waters rise in Appalachian highlands far to the west. Tributary branches course along a trellis of mountain valleys and ridge-gaps toward the rolling Piedmont. I stand downstream by the main channel, near the farthest inland reach of the sea. Here the Piedmont's crystalline bedrock, cut by Foundry Branch, by Rock Creek, and by the river itself at Great Falls and Mather Gorge, descends beneath the blanketing coastal plain. This is the *fall line*, where a Piedmont river widens to become a tidewater arm of Chesapeake Bay.

The changing lay of land and water is clear. I like to watch this river flow through time, at high tide and low, separating Maryland from Virginia. The Potomac has carried what some call the freight of history on its back. I am part of the river's load.

CALIFORNIA! WAS ALWAYS my immediate response to the question "where is home?" I'd go out of my way to deflect any tie to the District. How could such a place be home? Not with summer humidity fading clouds and sky-blue. Not with a land so flat and drab. Not with a city in decay and sometimes in flames. Certainly not with spit. I spent so much of my growing-up years trying to convince my parents to return west that I couldn't see what Washington meant to my father. Not until it was too late.

Both my parents are buried here. And I, though not born here, realize I exist because of this river, this city, and how it came to be.

At least five generations of paternal forebears made a home at the Potomac's fall line where a capital city grew. Earlier lives— indentured, enslaved, and free—may have come because of what colonists believed the cultivated tidewater and Piedmont lands could yield.

THE PARADOX THAT is our nation's capital struck me as from a blow on January 20, 2009. That day nearly two million people gathered to witness Senator Barack Obama become the forty-fourth president of the United States, the first African American in this office. My friend Kris and I were among them. Millions more who watched the events on television witnessed tradition and pageant: the oath of office taken on the Capitol steps, the new president's inaugural address, then the parade along Pennsylvania Avenue to the White House. Glimpses of monuments and memorials in downtown Washington may have been, for many, familiar reminders of national promise.

We'd taken an early 32 Metrobus to Foggy Bottom that bright morning, wind chill in the teens, to walk with an expectant crowd to the National Mall. This crowd differed in character and tone from all I'd known. Young parents carried toddlers in backpacks. Elderly walked with youth. Well-dressed affluence shared sidewalks with many more of poorer means. Strangers nodded and spoke to each other with kindness. I overheard a young woman lean down to tell the child whose hand she held, "Remember this day and be proud of who you are." Children of nearly every continent stood together.

It was then that I saw with a new clarity how Washington, D.C., is an invented place. For unlike capitals of most other nations, the District began far from the country's economic, intellectual, or cultural centers. Its origins arose instead from a political deal. The capital also harbored from its earliest days a "secret city" of free and enslaved African Americans—a secret city my father's people inhabited.

PUBLIC HISTORY TENDS to present the founding of the nation's capital in these terms: The Constitution authorized a district of up to ten miles square as the permanent seat of the new federal government. In July 1790, Congress passed the Residence Act, empowering President George Washington to choose a site along an eighty-mile stretch of the Potomac River "between the mouths of the Eastern Branch and the Connogochegue." An educational display at Mount Vernon emphasizes that "Washington took his authority a step further and set about personally overseeing every aspect of the project." Whether developed or not, the site would replace Philadelphia as the capital in 1800.

Yet public history often fails to mention the back story, the *why* behind this geography. Put simply, the first president wanted the capital embedded in the South, not too distant from his Virginia plantation. It was inconvenient if not difficult for a president who depended on enslaved workers—or any federal official in similar circumstances—to live in his desired and accustomed manner in a region antagonistic to it. With its Quaker heritage, Philadelphia was long known for abolitionist sentiments. A new law automatically manumitted any "slave" brought into Pennsylvania for more than six months. The permanent home for the federal government, in George Washington's mind, had to be located where slavery would remain unmolested.

The capital's placement and growth would also depend upon both local site and larger situation, the broader reaching social and economic contexts. For Washington, D.C., both site and situation came down to the Potomac River's fall line, where ancient, resistant bedrock of the Piedmont dips eastward beneath loose sediments of the coastal plain. At this inflection point Atlantic-flowing rivers leave their rockbound channels to meander as broader waterways on the tidewater plain. By tracing the fall line across rivers from Alabama to New Jersey, one can see the long line of settlements begun at a time when the power of moving water drove industry, and sailing ships were tools of commerce and war. In Georgia, Macon on the Ocmulgee River and Augusta on the Savannah. Columbia, South Carolina, on the Congaree. Richmond, Virginia, on the James. Philadelphia and Trenton on the Delaware. Colonial towns-now-cities began at the farthest inland reach of oceangoing vessels, the head of navigation.

George Washington's plantation lay along the Potomac below its fall line. He hoped canals and overland roads would make the river an artery of commerce connecting the western interior—"the Ohio countrie" beyond the mountains—and the trans-Atlantic world. Pittsburgh sat closer to the site he had in mind than it did to Philadelphia.

The new president stood somewhat in the background as his secretary of state and the leader of the House of Representatives, fellow Virginians Thomas Jefferson and James Madison, negotiated this plan. Jefferson later recounted the events coming down to a so-called dinner-table bargain with Secretary of the Treasury Alexander Hamilton. Whatever deals occurred behind the scenes in the end subverted Congressional authority and cut debate on alternative sites. The District of Columbia would grow from land ceded at and below the Potomac fall line.

Thus, in July of 1790, Congress voted by a narrow margin to move the capital from New York City to Philadelphia for a decade, until the chosen site could open for business. President Washington also sought a supplemental act to include Alexandria (in Virginia) and more of Maryland below the Eastern Branch (Anacostia River) to the authorized area. Vice President John Adams suggested that the value of the president's land had jumped "a thousand percent."

The first federal census, in 1790, counted more than half of the new nation's nearly seven hundred thousand souls held in bondage in just Virginia and Maryland. Of free African Americans, more than one-third lived in these two states.

My father's ancestors, my ancestors, have appeared on the scene by now. They may be part of the city's why, what, and how. Perhaps they've been here much longer. Traces of earlier lives remain as yet undiscovered. So, again, I fall back on history, hoping that in its relating I might come nearer to ghosts.

TOBACCO AGRICULTURE HAD defined the tidewater for nearly two centuries. Chesapeake exports exploded from a few thousand pounds in the 1610s to millions of pounds a few decades later. With Alexandria and Georgetown, the new District of Columbia included two thriving commercial ports, both homeports for ships

George Washington employed in the river trade. Downstream of Georgetown, on the Maryland side, the District also contained the small town sites of Hamburgh, near the mouth of Rock Creek, and Carrollsburg on the Eastern Branch. Woodlands, mosquito-infested tidal marshes, port towns, and cultivated fields of about twenty plantations and farms worked by enslaved laborers seeded the new federal city.

The President's House (later called the White House) would be built on David Burnes's tobacco plantation. The Capitol would rise on an estate owned by Daniel Carroll. Goose or Tiber Creek flowed where Constitution Avenue now runs, emptying into the Potomac River where the monument grounds now lie. The Navy Department would set up one of its six building yards near the mouth of the Eastern Branch. Here I make a mental note to return.

Visitors to the City of Washington early in the nineteenth century were often surprised. They found abandoned projects and partly built structures, shacks and stately manor houses scattered between fields and woods. Roads were muddy or dusty depending on the weather. "The city itself is unlike any other that was ever seen, straggling out hither and thither, with a small house or two a quarter of a mile from any other," Harriet Martineau recalled of her 1838 travels, "so that, in making calls 'in the city,' we had to cross ditches and stiles, and walk alternately on grass and pavements, and strike across a field to reach a street." Congress supposedly met between the harvest and next season's planting, to avoid sweltering summers when insect- and water-borne diseases were assured. Resignations and proposals to move the capital to a more hospitable location were proffered year after year after year.

"It is sometimes called the City of Magnificent Distances, but it might with greater propriety be termed the City of Magnificent Intentions," a young Charles Dickens observed on his 1842 visit. "Spacious avenues, that begin in nothing and lead nowhere;

streets, mile-long, that want only houses, roads, and inhabitants; public buildings that need but a public to be complete; and ornaments of great thoroughfares, which only lack great thoroughfares to ornament—are its leading features." Four decades after it began, Washington hadn't yet arrived.

AROUND THE NATION'S centennial, Frederick Douglass recalled with great "sorrow" that the capital's placement "was one of the greatest mistakes made by the fathers of the Republic," a mistake that "contained the seeds of civil war and disunion." For

> sandwiched between two of the oldest slave states, each of which was a nursery and a hot-bed of slavery; surrounded by a people accustomed to look upon the youthful members of a colored man's family as a part of the annual crop for the market; pervaded by the manners, morals, politics, and religion peculiar to a slaveholding community, the inhabitants of the National Capital were, from first to last, frantically and fanatically sectional. It was southern in all its sympathies and national only in name.

Douglass described himself "pretty roughly handled" by the controversy that followed. Yet he had simply spoken the truth. Washington was embedded where indentured and enslaved laborers had for two centuries brought the tidewater plain under cultivation. Congress had initially adopted for the District the laws of Maryland and Virginia "as they now exist," accepting a colonial act of the Maryland General Assembly that "all Negroes and other Slaves already Imported or hereafter to be Imported into this Province, and all Children now born or hereafter to be born of such Negroes and Slaves shall be Slaves during their natural lives." Thomas Jefferson, James Madison, James Monroe, Andrew

Jackson, John Tyler, James K. Polk, and Zachary Taylor staffed the White House with enslaved servants during their presidencies. Slavery would thread the District's daily business until the second year of the Civil War.

The irony wasn't lost on Irish poet Thomas Moore. Touring in 1801 he penned a few lines:

> Even here beside the proud Potomac's stream,
> . . . .
> Who can, with patience, for a moment see
> The medley mass of pride and misery,
> Of whips and charters, manacles and rights,
> Of slaving blacks and democratic whites . . .

AFRICAN AMERICANS ACCOUNTED for roughly a quarter to one-third of the capital's population at the turn of the nineteenth century. My father's people were likely among them.

Those enslaved outnumbered free five to one. They cleared sites for the imagined city. They built much of the Capitol, the President's House, and other projects public and private. Records of the Commissioners for the District of Columbia directed compensation to "owners" for "Negro hire" as quarrymen, sawyers, and stonecutters, as brick makers and layers, as carpenters, plasterers, roofers, painters, more. One voucher from February 1795 lists Miss Ann Digges being paid $52.33 "for Dick 5 months & Tom 6 months" for work on the Capitol. Most records omit the names of those who labored. More common are entries like this: Daniel Carroll of Duddington received $72.62 "for the hire of four sawyers" on September 29, 1800.

Acknowledged or not, the hands, strength, and skills of "Negro hire" fashioned building materials from outcrop and woods, from sand and mud, and then constructed a capital city. It may never be possible to know how many helped erect the iconic structures so visible on inauguration days. And working alongside them were those recently manumitted as well as freemen of color who had never felt the shackles of bondage. One receipt shows a "Negro" named Rhode Butler paid sixty-seven cents on April 2, 1801.

After the British attack in 1814, gangs of "Negro" workers would again be hired to rebuild the Capitol, White House, and other buildings. In later years they laid foundations of the monument to the first president. Two centuries would pass before Congress publicly acknowledged these builders of the capital city.

. . .

Until my thirties I believed that my father's sister, brother, and theirs were his living family. All born in Washington. Aunt Rhoda's daughters, Cissie and Little Rhoda, were the only cousins on his side I knew. Only Aunt Rhoda told me of our past, and just two specific things: The Savoys were never slaves; they owned land in Silver Spring, Maryland, just north of the city. I was about twelve when she spoke these words in that deliberate tone of hers, old enough to know I'd better pay attention even if meaning eluded me. Aunt Rhoda is long dead, too.

A few years ago I confided to Cissie my longing to know of origins. Of who we were to each other. Of who we were to these tidewater and Piedmont lands. I wanted to respond to her mother's declarations not so much to verify their truth as to find a tangible thread that would place me, explain me in time and space. I had little else to grasp.

"Oh, you need to meet Buddy," she replied.

"Buddy? Who's he?"

"He's your cousin. He's working on the family genealogy."

Why I hadn't met or even known of cousin Buddy I can't say beyond chalking it up to the residue of family silences. Cissie took me to his house that afternoon, a first cousin introducing me to a third.

Buddy had traced the Savoy line to our third great-grandmother Eliza. She appears in paper records because she lived in the home of Timothy Winn, purser of the Washington Navy Yard from 1815 until his death in 1836. Winn controlled the yard's contracting and procurement when it might have been the city's largest employer. Buddy invited me along to search through Winn's estate documents in the National Archives. What I remember most of our visit is the smell.

Once opened the archival box released the mustiness of age. Our white gloves picked up a fine gray-tan dust as we oh-so-gently handled page after page. Buddy took half the contents, reading Winn's will. I took the estate inventory. Along with parcels of land, a house, and household items of a learned, traveled, and comfortably situated man—carpeting, silver, mahogany sideboards, desks, library cases—Winn's personal estate included various stocks, globes of the world, a large *New Map of the United States* by Mitchell, and copies of both the Declaration of Independence and Washington's Farewell Address set in gilded frames. She appeared in the third to last entry on the last page of an inventory valued at $16,824.37. "Eliza Savoy $300." Below her, below other "servants" listed, the subscribers certified the justness and truth of this "inventory and valuation of the goods, chattels, and personal estate of Timothy Winn late of Washington County."

The quiet of that room caught my breath. Our great-great-great-grandmother was inked in by name as property of a dead man, to be disposed of by the terms of his will. It seemed that Aunt Rhoda might have erred in at least this case.

The will wasn't what we expected, if I could admit to having any expectation. Timothy Winn had made a special provision for "my Servant Woman Lizy, or Eliza Savoy" and two sons. She and another aging man were never "to be sold, nor be set free on any account whatever. I have too much regard for them to set them free to provide for & support themselves in their old age, after having had their faithful services for the best part of their lives. They must be comfortably & well provided for & kindly treated & supported & receive every indulgence compatible with their situation."

Of Eliza's "situation" we imagined a great deal. Of her origins and her fate we still know little. Nor do we know the father of her boys, though we have suspicions. Eliza's son Edward and his young wife Elizabeth Butler Savoy appear in the 1850 and 1860 censuses in Washington City as free mulattoes.

I know that many people of color in this city as elsewhere were of mixed African, European, and/or Native ancestry. That many "passed" to become "white." That many did not. The color line was crossed multiple times to my knowledge in my father's family. I was reminded of this all too well on meeting two cousins on one visit to Washington not long ago. Pat and I share a great-grandfather, Edward Augustine Savoy. She is a gracious woman with warm, chestnut-brown skin. Also a gracious woman, Sally and I share a great-great-grandmother Lipscomb on my paternal grandmother's side. Pale of complexion and sharply featured, Sally's great-grandfather chose whiteness and left Cumberland County, Virginia. Though also pale and similarly featured, his sister, my great-grandmother, remained "mulatto." Because of choices made almost a century and a half ago, Sally came into this world, and has lived her life, as a white woman. I have not. Lipscombs still reside in Cumberland. I know, too, that Savoys and Butlers live downstream of the District in Prince George's and Charles counties, Maryland. Some claim Piscataway heritage. I must meet them.

• • •

Tobacco crops quickly exhausted soil fertility. So Chesapeake planters often sold or hired out their human "property" once the Constitutional ban on importing captive Africans went into effect in 1808. They would take advantage of the booming inter-state trade as commercial cotton spread across the Deep South. The nation's capital soon became a large market depot. Even free-born African Americans risked being kidnapped as "runaways" in what abolitionists and later historians referred to as "the very seat and center of the slave trade."

Vestiges of slavery's landscapes and architecture still lie in plain sight in the city, though the holding pens are long gone. Some of the most notorious markets and pens stood along the Mall where so many would come for Barack Obama's inaugurations. One might have operated by Seventh Street and Maryland Avenue SW, another nearby at Eighth Street and what is now Independence Avenue. The Hirshhorn and Air & Space museums sit just a block from the sites.

Members of the House and Senate often saw from their win-dows, as New York Congressman James Tallmadge did in 1819, "a trafficker in human flesh" driving chained and handcuffed men, women, and children by the tip of a whip. President Madison's private secretary, Edward Coles, reproached his employer "by con-gratulating him, as the Chief of our great Republic, that he was not then accompanyed by a Foreign Minister, & thus saved the deep mortification of witnessing such a revolting sight in the presence of the representative of a nation, less boastful perhaps of its regard for the rights of man, but more observant of them."

Yes, the pens and most other signs of urban slavery were torn down after the Civil War. But one can still see outbuildings next to stately residences scattered across the city and in Alexandria. De-catur House stands by the northwest corner of Lafayette Square, across from the White House. Its second owner, a prominent trafficker in human flesh, built a two-story structure behind his home as quarters for those enslaved. A few blocks southeast of the Capitol sit what remains of The Maples or Maple Grove plantation: a large brick house, quarters, and other outbuildings from the 1790s. A new residential development of upscale flats, duplexes, and townhouses called The Maples has incorporated these structures. The namesake grove of silver maples is long gone.

LITTLE REMAINS OF the antebellum landscapes of free people of color. Their growing presence so alarmed mayors and city councils that the first of a series of Black codes was enacted in 1808, shortly after the capital opened for business. Designed to limit the movement of African Americans, "loose, idle, disorderly" persons, and those "without visible means of support," as well as reduce their influx to the city, the codes also aimed to check "unruly slaves" through enforced curfews and public conduct rules. As restraints on life and livelihood tightened, the codes imposed ever harsher indignities. A pass was needed to move about after 10 p.m. Dances and parties required permits. Alcohol couldn't be purchased after nightfall. Intermarriage between "colored persons and white persons" held dire penalties. Suffrage was out of the question. Anything to abate what many white citizens perceived as a threat. If free people of color could enjoy "privileges" in the capital denied them elsewhere in the South, who knew when the floodgates could be closed!

Code amendments called for "free colored persons" to register with the city government and carry certificates of freedom at all times or be subject to arrest or capture as runaways. Soon they had to present to the mayor, in person, not only papers of freedom but also vouchers signed by white citizens guaranteeing their good character and solvency. They had to post a "peace bond." By 1827 the bond amount had increased to five hundred dollars and required a guarantee by two "respected" white men. Then Congress barred all African Americans from the Capitol grounds unless there on official business. Segregation ruled in death as well as life, as burial grounds separated mortal remains by race.

Still, these codes weren't severe enough to keep free men and women of color from seeking refuge within the capital city. Their numbers continued to grow—by new arrivals, by manumission, and by self-purchase—such that the 1830 census counted more free than enslaved for the first time. White citizens expressed great interest in having "dusky" immigrants colonize Liberia. This "scheme simultaneously salved tender consciences," writes historian Constance Green, "and allayed apprehensions about whether any American city, the capital above all, could assimilate a large Negro population."

Most Black Washingtonians had different ideas. In the spring of 1831 a large group gathered at the African Methodist Episcopal Church and formally declared that "the soil that gave us birth is our only true and veritable home." Similar words would be voiced until the Civil War. My father's people might have spoken among them.

The possibility of revolt frightened some white citizens. So many free people of color roaming about, they thought, could only put ideas into the heads of those enslaved. Nat Turner's rebellion in August 1831, less than two hundred miles south in Virginia, didn't help.

Rising hysteria broke in the sweltering heat of August 1835 after local newspapers reported the capital harbored its own version of Nat Turner. A mob of several hundred white youth and men began with the Epicurean Eating House owned by Beverly Snow, a free "mulatto," then went on to loot, vandalize, or destroy schools, homes, businesses, and places of worship. Following the "Snow Storm" or "Snow Riot" the city council cracked down not on the mob but on those attacked. It passed ever more restrictive codes. Free residents of color could no longer run a tavern or restaurant. The peace bond was raised to one thousand dollars and required the assurance of five respected white men. "We have already too many free negroes and mulattoes in this city, and the policy of our corporate authorities should tend to the diminution of this insolent class," wrote one anonymous citizen in the local press. "If they wish to live here, let them become subordinates and laborers, as nature has designed."

Yet prohibitions would collapse. The work done by residents of color was needed. As domestic servants, waiters and cooks, carpenters, bricklayers, oystermen, blacksmiths, washerwomen, hackmen and carters, livery-stable hands, shoemakers and tailors, messengers, general laborers. This list goes on.

Though the city council continued tinkering with the codes, nearly one-third of the District's inhabitants were people of color by the mid-1840s. Most of them, more than thirteen thousand, were free. Months before the opening volleys at Fort Sumter, the 1860 census would count 5 percent of the nation's African American population as free. Those living in Washington outnumbered those in bondage by nearly four to one.

To know that ancestors inhabited this history *and* this place yet to find little of their lives gnaws, a deep hunger. Had some lived among tribal societies who witnessed those first English ships sail up the Chesapeake Bay? Perhaps. Had they come as tobacco plantations grew along the tidewater plain? I suspect so. Were they deposited in this city by the intrigue that moved the capital to the Potomac River? I think so. Did they come to define their own lives as free people within the antebellum code structure? Yes. The 1860 Federal Census lists my great-great-grandfather Edward Savoy as a "laborer," my great-great-grandmother Elizabeth a "washerwoman."

*

NEITHER SLAVERY NOR the business of human trafficking existed easily in the nation's capital. Abolitionists maintained that Congress could ban both given its jurisdiction over the federal city. The counterargument ran that Maryland and Virginia never would have ceded land for the capital if slavery weren't protected by law as it was in those states. The first issue of William Lloyd Garrison's *The Liberator*, from January 1, 1831, ran front-page articles on the D.C. trade.

Abolitionists petitioned Congress repeatedly. Even members of the city council who held people in bondage protested the District trade because too much of the "merchandise" was handled by non-resident dealers who took profits out of the city. Fed-up Southern Congressmen passed a "gag rule" in 1836 tabling anti-slavery petitions. Eight years would elapse before its repeal. Fearful traders, port merchants, and planters soon pressured Congress to cede Alexandria back to Virginia and Virginia law in 1846. When the ban on importing "slaves" into Washington for sale eventually did pass as part of the Compromise of 1850, interstate traffic simply shifted across the river.

And white Washingtonians tended to be quiet about their own bondspeople, especially after an Illinois congressman named Abraham Lincoln introduced an unsuccessful bill to abolish District slavery altogether in January 1849. Only in April of 1862, as the war entered its second year, would a Republican-controlled Congress end the institution in the nation's capital.

The local anti-slavery community formed one of the southern cells of organized activity by setting up escape routes and depots between Washington and Philadelphia, New York, and other points north. This history I knew from reading over the years. Only by chance did I learn that ancestors were part of it. A single sentence

PLACING WASHINGTON, D.C., AFTER THE INAUGURATION   177

left a trace in an old article on the "free Negro population" of Washington: "Elizabeth Savoy, wife of Edward Savoy, a successful caterer, worked with the underground railway and helped slaves make their way northward to Canada and freedom." One sentence in an article with no noted source. The author, long dead, apparently left no research files. Yet twenty-five words revealed more about the kind of woman my great-great-grandmother was than "washerwoman" on a census ever could. Her husband made a "successful" living at a time when most respectable jobs were closed to free men of color.

A will and estate inventory listing three ancestors. Census records enumerating others. Death certificates for a few. A chance note in a journal article. Land records from Silver Spring, Maryland, "lost" long ago.

One Savoy line ends with me.

• • •

I first visited Woodlawn Cemetery on a January day that defined bleakness. In hand a registry listing buried family, given to me by Mr. Paul Sluby, a local authority and the country's first certified African American genealogist. Edward and Elizabeth Savoy lie there, with her mother and many of their children. Lot 81, Section C.

Although I had no map, I wanted to turn to solid ground. I'd walk each and every row if need be to find their marker. My friend Kris joined me, eager to help.

We found the iron entrance gate locked. Through it we could see large upright stone monuments near the base of a broad hill to the west. They were too distant to read. Disappointment nearly turned us away until we found we could squeeze through a gap between the brick gatepost and chain-link fence.

Weeds had claimed the driveway long ago. Washouts had taken their share, too. We walked up pebbly channels to the granite monuments. Langston. Bruce. Murray. Names I'd heard of. Other gravestones were on the hill, too. Marble, granite, sandstone—most lay toppled at every angle in jumbled piles as if they'd been ripped up and deposited by passing waves. Many lay partly sunken into earth. Others were broken or upside down. Shrubs and hardwood saplings encroached from the cemetery's edges over now-anonymous graves. Grass bowed toward us in a downslope wind.

I am drawn to old graveyards. To wander row after row wondering over inscribed epitaphs. Births. Deaths. To imagine who these people might have been *in between*. I thought we would do the same here until a stone carved SAVOY came into sight. My unspoken wish was to be guided by old murmurs, by voices calling from beneath the sod. I had to pay respects to those who anticipated me.

AT REST or IN MEMORY OF could be read on stones whose names were covered by soil. In the wind-rattle of dry winter grass it was easy to wonder if such memory still existed. When last had a mourner come to visit any of my buried family?

We roamed that hill for two hours or more. And we were watched. One observer used binoculars from a house that backed against the fenced northern edge. Fifteen or twenty vocal crows gathered on the limbs of an ivy-choked oak on the hilltop.

Every "maybe over here" ended with nothing. We couldn't even find Section C.

When we at last descended the eroding path to the gate, my mind caught on one thought: This cemetery is an eddy left behind by currents of passing generations. This cemetery is an eddy left behind. . . . My stomach churned with the flint-gray sky.

Paul Sluby later told me that thirty-six thousand people were laid to rest on that hillside, several thousand of them, white and

Black, reinterred from older cemeteries that were built over as the city grew. Woodlawn was established in 1895, the year Frederick Douglass died—his home at Cedar Hill sits less than three miles away in Anacostia. In those days the cemetery's acres lay in open country. The last interments at Woodlawn took place years ago. Buried with little trace are enough people to populate a town.

Cousin Pat and I returned the following winter. This time we had an 1897 plan showing lots and sections. Section C lay high on the hill, near the crow-tree. We walked around and over what had to be Lot 81.

A CEMETERY OVERGROWN and eroded. Its markers disturbed. Its caretakers volunteers who kept the city from declaring the land abandoned. The National Register of Historic Places listed Woodlawn in 1996, yet the struggle to raise funds for tending the grounds has been constant.

Mortal remains of some of the most prominent and noteworthy African Americans of the last century and a half lie there. Blanche Kelso Bruce, born into slavery, became the first to serve a full term in the Reconstruction Senate. (Almost a century would pass before another African American would be a U.S. senator.) John Mercer Langston, namesake of Langston City, Oklahoma, was perhaps the first Black man elected to public office in this country. An Oberlin College graduate, he served in the House of Representatives from Virginia after the Civil War, and established the law department at Howard University. Both men were respected enough to hold public posts for the capital city: President Grant selecting Langston for the District's Board of Health; President Garfield appointing Bruce as register of the U.S. Treasury. The size of their upright monuments reflects the importance of these men in life. There are others, too. From Reconstruction through the New Deal, men and women buried at Woodlawn broke barriers meant to keep them "in their place." Here lie members of Congress, physicians, educators, artists, civic leaders, lawyers, and business-people of note. Lyric soprano Lillian Evanti was the first African American to sing with a major European opera company.

To preserve a burial ground is an act of remembrance. Neglect may reflect many things: commitment but lack of means; amnesia or apathy; perhaps forces more complex and sinister.

The capital and its architecture of urban slavery inscribed the geography of race from day one. Woodlawn Cemetery was established to serve mainly the needs of African American Washingtonians, many of them longtime residents whose families formed the core of the city's antebellum free population. At a time when segregation followed one from cradle to grave, these people provided dignified burial places for their own.

So many of those interred hadn't been "put in their place" in life. On Woodlawn's hill, I couldn't but wonder if buried memories somehow meant they were "put in their place" in death. Too few current residents of the surrounding neighborhood, African Americans also, know of those lying here—even though a District congresswoman helped organize a clean-up day in 2013 that brought together volunteers from the D.C. National Guard, the cemetery's caretaker association, and families of those interred.

Loss of memory looms for any cemetery that is no longer active. But it's hard for me to imagine one with the remains of white congressmen, physicians, educators, artists, civic leaders, lawyers, and business-people of note sharing a similar fate.

At what point does a burial ground lose its sanctity?

• • •

I stand again at the bank of the Potomac River, under an evening sun. Muddy waters course by, following a week of rain.

Washington, D.C. As unmoored as driftwood in this swift current, I never felt at home in my father's home after we left California.

Yet I, like my father, am a child of this river, of these tidewater and Piedmont lands, of a capital sited on the fall line. Those of my blood might have planted and harvested tobacco that drove the commerce of Chesapeake colonies. Ancestors might have helped build this capital city—or laid foundations for a monument to the man who brought the seat of government South. Might. May. Fragments yield few clear answers. A woman valued at three hundred dollars. Her daughter-in-law aiding the Underground Railroad. Words declared by free "colored" residents that the soil that gave them birth is their "only true and veritable home." A patch of unmarked burial ground on a windswept hill.

Odysseus said, *I belong in the place of my departure and I belong in the place that is my destination.* To reach from California, the place of my birth, to this place of deeper origins, where roots began to twine, is a belated coming home.

The past and its landscapes lie close. They linger in eroded, scattered pieces, both becoming and passing into what I am, what I think we are. Perhaps the shadows of unnumbered years have touched me in choices made, in backward yearnings, in fears as well as dreams. Perhaps they form the natural and unnatural histories of my soul.

Names like Foggy Bottom and Rock Creek remain well known and used, while others—Hamburgh, Tiber Creek—have fallen out of living memory. But Tiber Creek's waters still try to flow to this river, trickling through a filled-in channel and a sewer buried beneath pavement, concrete, and city buildings. Waters remember.

At the bank of the Potomac River I watch ripples rise, sun-jeweled for an instant, then disappear into the current. I must continue the search.

EPILOGUE: AT CROWSNEST PASS

Glacier. Waterton Lakes. Banff, Kootenay, Yoho. Jasper. The backbone of the continent winds through or borders these Rocky Mountain parks. From northern Montana up along the crenulated divide between southern Alberta and British Columbia, range after range lift strata laid down over a billion years, from distant Precambrian seas to coal swamps formed when dinosaurs reigned.

Like the more ancient Appalachians, these mountains also arose in response to collisions at the continent's edge. But here, compressive forces in a tectonic-plated world pushed from the Pacific west, rupturing bedrock and shoving broken slabs thousands of feet thick up and over one another to the east. Terrain that once spread toward the western horizon was squeezed and stacked along great thrust faults to a fraction of its original extent. Such imbricated lithic waves are called a fold-and-thrust belt.

I came to these mountains as a graduate student in search of an interval of great environmental change. Tropical seas had once covered much of the continent in the remote past. But at times the oceanic realm became so starved of oxygen that many sea creatures couldn't survive. One such episode occurred here almost 360 million years ago, marking a boundary in geologic time—between the Devonian and Mississippian periods. The telltale sign of catastrophe could be found in range after range: thin black shale punctuating massive Bahamas-like limestone. The facies, the *aspects* of the rocks, told much. Most sections lay on high mountain ridges, but not all.

The continental divide can be subtle. Crowsnest Highway climbs an incline so gentle that a speeding motorist might wonder, *was that it?*, long after departing southern British Columbia to enter Alberta. But the roadcut at Crowsnest Pass, on the flank of Sentry Mountain, offered a rare view. There my hammer's flat edge split apart black shale laminae, exposing to light and air the burial grounds of a long-dead sea. Pieces smelled of oil. Glossy shapes lay scattered on some smooth black surfaces. Barely an inch in length, these compressed carbon films resembled a four-year-old's drawing of fish. My field partner and I had seen nothing like them before, and many samples returned with us at the end of the season.

Invertebrate paleontologists scratched their heads over these enigmatic fossils, suggesting they might be plants. Paleobotanists scratched their heads, too, proposing soft-bodied metazoans. Simon Conway Morris had another idea. Known for describing the bizarre fossils of the Burgess Shale, an older deposit on another mountain thrust sheet to the north, he thought we had found a "new" taxon. These soft-body remains bore no compelling affinity with any other recognized organism alive or extinct. No protist, no fungus, no alga, no vascular plant, no animal. Kingdom, phylum, class, order, family—all were uncertain.

So they joined the ranks of problematic fossils, those pariahs of paleontology that don't neatly fit into narratives of evolution. Their mere existence highlighted the mysteries of life's past. The Crowsnest Pass specimens were named a new genus and species— *Libodiscus* (for the teardrop shape), *ascitus* (for the strange, alien appearance). Best described as *incertae sedis*, *Libodiscus ascitus* gen. et sp. nov. lies in an uncertain position, without assurance of relationship. *Incertae sedis*. Homeless. Alien.

*

THE JOURNEYS THAT once-living organisms embark on toward the fossil record, few rarely complete. Happy accidents brought these remains within my reach. Of their escaping decay on a quiet sea floor too inhospitable for hungry scavengers and most bacteria. Of thrust faults upheaving bedrock once deeply buried. Of erosion cutting into ranges such that a highway could be built along a path of least resistance—yet not dissecting so far as to destroy the outcrop. Of my hammer splitting the right shale layers.

Annals of the past in these mountains lie incomplete and fragmented. Millions of years may be lost in the gaps between black-shale laminae so thin as to be pages of a book of night. Time condensed and time eroded; punctuated discontinuity rather than layered continuity. Then mountain building ruptured the bedrock terrain. I didn't realize it, but we—fossils and woman—arrived to meet that day in the field, a chance moment of exposure together.

A dear friend once asked me if history is more about forgetting and deletion than about remembering and completion. The past I've emerged from is also broken and pitted by gaps left by silences stretched across generations. By losses of language and voice. By human displacements. By immeasurable dimensions of lives compressed and deflated. And by dismembering narratives of who "we" are to each other in this land. Illusions of rootlessness in one's own home could only grow in such depleted and contested soil.

To inhabit this country is to be marked by residues of its still unfolding history, a history weighted by tangled ideas of "race" and of the land itself. And because of this I've lived as *incertae sedis*, estrangement beginning with an eight-year-old's wish for a place before race. Even then I suspected the possibility of extinction crept close.

Trace. Active search. Path taken. Track or vestige of what once was. These narrative journeys have crossed textured lands seeking both life marks and home. From twisted terrain within the San Andreas Fault zone to "Indian Territory," from Point Sublime to burial grounds, from a South Carolina plantation to the U.S.–Mexico border and U.S. capital. Their confluence *articulates*—that is, helps me both join together and give clearer expression to—the unvoiced past in my life. *Re-membering* is an alternative to extinction.

Home indeed lies among the ruins and shards that surround us all.

ACKNOWLEDGMENTS

If each of our lives is an instant, like a camera shutter opening then closing, what can we make of our place in the world, of the latent image, for that instant? What do accumulated instants mean? This book began as a search for some answers. I soon learned that *re-membering* a fragmented past-into-present could never be solitary work. The spirit, faith, and guidance of so many fill these pages and it is impossible to acknowledge all to whom I owe a debt of gratitude.

With great love and respect I dedicate *Trace* to my parents: to my father who died before I could know him, or the questions, and to my mother who died as I made the journey. *Trace* is also an offering of respect to the American land and to those, like my father and writer Louis Owens, who struggled to negotiate the indeterminate, liminal terrain of "mixed" heritage and write toward understanding and survival.

Heartfelt thanks go to John Elder, John Lemly, Kris Bergbom, Karen Remmler, Helen Whybrow, Dorinda Dallmeyer, Danyelle O'Hara, Scott Russell Sanders, Gerald Vizenor, and Curt Meine, who read draft after draft over the years, not only providing astute editorial insight but believing in me and my words when I didn't. To John Daniel, who sensed enough promise in rough words read aloud a decade ago to offer to introduce me to Jack Shoemaker, his editor, when the manuscript—and I—were ready. To Terry Tempest Williams who, after an exhausting day of travel and a reading on a book tour two decades ago, listened well into the night to a stranger struggling to find words for her own unspoken hunger.

I have benefitted from ideas sparked and connections made at gatherings of writers and thinkers:

The people I met at the last Art of the Wild broadened my sense of possibility. Founding director Jack Hicks's encouragement to avoid what he called "derivative" nature writing stayed with me. A conversation with Alison Deming kindled both friendship and our work together as coeditors of *The Colors of Nature*. Another conversation with Barbara Ras led to my working with her and Barry Lopez on *Home Ground: Language for an American Landscape* as well as my own collection *Bedrock*. Al Young and Gary Nabhan became supporters and cheerleaders. And Louis Owens became the catalyst. His writings on "mixedblood messages," our deep friendship, and his death pushed me to find language for what I had been unable to articulate.

I also warmly thank Carolyn Servid and Doric Mechau of the Island Institute; H. Emerson (Chip) Blake and Jennifer Sahn of the Orion Society and Wildbranch Writing Workshop; Steve Costa, Kate Levinson, and colleagues of the Geography of Hope conferences; the Glen Brook gathering of writers; and friends met at all of these places. A residency at the Mesa Refuge, in California's San Andreas Fault zone, allowed me to return home.

And sincere thanks go to the Center for Whole Communities for being a crucible of ideas at the intersection of conservation and social justice. Peter Forbes, Helen Whybrow, Ginny McGinn, and fellow board members (Danyelle O'Hara, John Elder, Gil Livingston, Tom Wessels, Scott Chaskey, Carolyn Finney, Julian Agyeman, Melissa Nelson, Torri Estrada, Hal Colston, Polly Hoppin, David Grant, and Kesha Ram) were all keen colleagues and teachers.

So many people welcomed me on my cross-country journeys, offering hospitality or guidance that allowed me to gain a firm grounding:

In the Arizona borderlands: Alison Deming, Joni Adamson, Steven Smith, William (Pat) O'Brien, Chip Colwell-Chanthaphonh, T. J. Ferguson, Steven Smith, Teresa Leal, Hermalene Wick-Curran, Chris Reid (Pinal County Historical Society Museum), Steve Hoza, Sigrid Maitrejean (Pimeria Alta Historical Society and Museum), Holly Richter (The Nature Conservancy), Herb Stevens (San Carlos Apache Cultural Center), Charles Hancock, Alexis Clark, Joseph "Ike" Dent, Kate Schmidli and Steve Gregory (Fort Huachuca Museum), Christine Seliga and Alexandria Caster (Arizona Historical Society), Bob Vint, Simmons Buntin, Steve and Karen Strom, Steve Boyle, and Nathan Loveland.

In South Carolina: Dorinda Dallmeyer, John Lane, Becky Slayton (Spartanburg County Historical Association), and staff of the South Caroliniana Library at the University of South Carolina.

In Oklahoma: Mrs. M. Joan Matthews and Mrs. Henrietta Hicks (Boley), and Bettye Black of the Melvin B. Tolson Black Heritage Center at Langston University.

In Washington, D.C.: My paternal cousins (Pat Wright, Buddy Rogers, Sylvia Rachele Hudson (Cissie), and Sally Phillips), Paul and Pat Sluby, Jeanette and Jean Pablo, Alan Spears, Mary McHenry, William Holton, Alice Harris, Bill Branch, Jennifer and Beto Torres, and Sue Richardson.

In Wisconsin: Penny Gill for the gift of time on Madeline Island; Curt Meine, Buddy Huffaker, Jeannine Richards, and colleagues at the Aldo Leopold Foundation; and Bob Krumenaker, Susan Edwards, and Terry Ball.

In Massachusetts: Robert Romer and Barbara Mathews for background on Deerfield, and Judi Urquhart of the Wôpanâak Language Reclamation Project.

My institution, Mount Holyoke College, has supported me in many ways—from sabbaticals to dynamic exchanges of ideas across disciplinary borders. Colleagues in the departments of Environmental Studies and Geology & Geography, and across the college, have been generous sounding boards. My deep gratitude goes to all of my students over the years. I've been honored to be their teacher and grateful to be their student. I add special thanks to the Class of 2002 who, in the uncertain wake of September 11, 2001, taught me to embrace the experiences, dreams, and hopes that stayed with me from childhood to womanhood.

For generosity, candor, and encouragement that kept me from throwing this work away, I am indebted to John Lemly, John Elder, Kris Bergbom, John Daniel, Terry Tempest Williams, Alison Hawthorne Deming, Gerald Vizenor, Louis Owens, Scott Russell Sanders, C. S. Manegold, Helen Whybrow, Karen Remmler, Curt Meine, Danyelle O'Hara, Dorinda Dallmeyer, Al Young, John Calderazzo, Tom Wessels, Julian Agyeman, Alan Spears, John McPhee, Simmons Buntin, John Tallmadge, Carolyn Servid, Kathleen Dean Moore, Catherine Corson, Michelle Markley, Donna McKeever, Gayle Pemberton, Penny Gill, Don O'Shea, Bob and Fi Herbert, Meggin McIntosh, Elizabeth Hemley, Sandy Johnson, Carol Drexler, Samuel Gladstone, Lisa Brooks, Chantal Norrgard, Jack Hicks, Scott Chaskey, John Lane, Alan Weisman, Sandra Postel, David Abram, Patrick Thomas, Nikky Finney, Carolyn Finney, Mistinguette Smith, Peter Forbes, Ginny McGinn, Brooke Hecht, Paul Sluby, Brooke Thomas, Barbara Ras, Ann Zwinger, Gil Livingston, Peter Sauer, Chip Blake, Jennifer Sahn, Aina Barten, Kim Leeder, Barbara Bosworth, Patricia Klindienst, Julia Frankenbach, Reed Hudson, Lisa Hupp, Emma Singer, Isobel Arthen, Aileen Suzara, Salma Monani, Jennifer García Peacock, Elise Cavicchi, Nina Payne, Ron Welburn, Gabrielle Tayac, Joan Grenier, John Hadden, Mark Leach, Michael McDermott, Robin Kimmerer,

Audrey Peterman, Drew Lanham, Michael Marx, Rie Hachiyanagi, Heath Atchley, Eldridge and Judy Moores, Jillian McLeod, Steve Roof, David Smith, Mrs. Sharon Koenig, Mrs. Pyle, Dianne Glave, Molly Sturges, Gary Nabhan, Julie Williams, Beverly East, Lorenza Muñoz, Sonia Shah, SueEllen Campbell, Doug Wheat, Deb Martin, Giovanna Di Chiro, Leah Glasser, Carole DeSanti, Gail Hornstein, Lois Brown, Anita Harris, Eric Mountjoy, Carrie Mae Weems, and more. The list is long and, with apologies, incomplete.

I also thank Jack Weatherford for a deeper exploration into the land of names. And the editors of *Terrain.org*, the *Gettysburg Review*, *Georgia Review*, and *Orion*, and where rough elements of this book first appeared.

Finally, I can't express enough gratitude to my colleagues at Counterpoint Press, in particular my editor Jack Shoemaker and Jane Vandenburgh. Thanks go to Megan Fishmann, Rolph Blythe, Claire Shalinsky, Corinne Kalasky, Kelly Winton, Sharon Wu, Charlie Winton, Debbie Berne, Mikayla Butchart, Irene Barnard, Joe Goodale, Deborah Kenmore, Matt Hoover, Kelli Adams, Steven Genise, Janelle Ludowise, Elyse Strongin and Neuwirth & Associates for the magic they work. I was born in Berkeley, California. Now this book, which I've been coming to all my life, has emerged with their help from my birthplace.

Many people had a hand in shaping *Trace*, yet I take full responsibility for any omissions or errors that remain. I hope readers will sense the respect and hope that inform these pages.

END NOTES

PROLOGUE: THOUGHTS ON A FROZEN POND

Loren Eiseley, *The Immense Journey* (New York: Random House, 1957).

THE VIEW FROM POINT SUBLIME

To Dutton the view from the point: Clarence Dutton, "The Panorama from Point Sublime" in *Tertiary History of the Grand Cañon District* (Washington: Government Printing Office, 1882; reprinted by the University of Arizona Press, 2001), 141.

Reference to "pioneer tourism entrepreneurs" and early North Rim roads in Michael F. Anderson, *Polishing the Jewel: An Administrative History of Grand Canyon National Park* (Grand Canyon: Grand Canyon Association Monograph No. 11, 2000), 21. http://www.nps.gov/grca/historyculture/adhigrca.htm.

Reference to motorists exceeding rail passengers in the summer of 1925 and thereafter: Anderson, *Polishing the Jewel*, 24.

On García López de Cárdenas's party reaching the South Rim in 1540 in Pedro de Castañeda de Nájera, translated by George Parker Winship, *The Journey of Francisco Vásquez de Coronado 1540–1542* (San Francisco: The Grabhorn Press, 1933; republished by Dover Publications, 1990), 22–23.

Clarence Dutton understood how easily one could be tricked: Dutton, *Tertiary History*, 149–50.

Although *Tertiary History* is Monograph 2 of the U.S. Geological Survey, it was actually the first of the monographs to be published. See Chester Longwell, "Clarence Edward Dutton, 1841–1912: A Biographic Memoir": National Academy of Sciences (1958), 137–38.

"The lover of nature": Dutton, *Tertiary History*, 141–42.

For more on Major Clarence Dutton and the Grand Canyon, see Dutton, *Tertiary History*, 140–56; Clarence Dutton, *Atlas to Accompany the Monograph on the Tertiary History of the Grand Cañon District* (Washington: Government Printing Office, 1882); Barbara Morehouse, *A Place Called Grand Canyon: Contested Geographies* (Tucson: University of Arizona Press, 1996); Mark Neumann, *On the Rim: Looking for the Grand Canyon* (Minneapolis: University of Minnesota Press, 1999); Stephen Pyne, *How the Canyon Became Grand: A Short History* (New York: Viking Penguin, 1998).

For Wallace Stegner on Clarence Dutton, see Stegner, *Beyond the Hundredth Meridian: John Wesley Powell and the Second Opening of the West* (Boston: Houghton Mifflin, 1954. Reprinted by the University of Nebraska Press, 1982), 173–74.

For Immanuel Kant's views on the sublime, see his 1790 *Critique of Judgment* (Kritik der Urteilskraft); also Paul Outka, *Race and Nature from Transcendentalism to the Harlem Renaissance* (New York: Palgrave Macmillan, 2008), 16–20.

W. E. B. Du Bois wrote of his visit to the Grand Canyon, as well as Acadia, Maine, in the essay "Of Beauty and Death" in *Darkwater: Voices from Within the Veil* (New York: Harcourt, Brace, 1920). Vivid descriptions of nature stand alongside accounts of why "Jim Crow" racism discouraged African Americans from traveling to such parks. The 1920 edition can be found at http://www.webdubois.org/wdb-darkwater.html.

PROVENANCE NOTES

The Sand Creek Massacre National Historic Site, the first park unit with *massacre* in its name, was dedicated on April 28, 2007, in southeastern Colorado. For a study of the meanings of Sand Creek in American history and memory, controversies over efforts to remember the massacre, oral history as a form of knowledge, and the ongoing significance of the massacre site to Cheyenne and Arapaho peoples, see Ari Kelman, *A Misplaced Massacre: Struggling over the Memory of Sand Creek* (Cambridge: Harvard University Press, 2013). The aftermath of the massacre still stirs controversy. History Colorado, the new museum in Denver, closed its Sand Creek exhibit in 2013 amid complaints and protests from many sides.

Information on African Americans enslaved in the five nations on pp. 62–71 in Quintard Taylor, *In Search of the Racial Frontier: African Americans in the American West, 1528–1990* (New York: W. W. Norton, 1998). Taylor considers the establishment of Black towns in Indian and Oklahoma territories on pp. 143–52. Additional information on Langston City and Boley from the Black Heritage Center archives at Langston University and the Oklahoma Historical Society's Encyclopedia of Oklahoma History and Culture (http://digital. library.okstate.edu/encyclopedia/).

ALIEN   LAND   ETHIC: THE DISTANCE BETWEEN

Selections quoted from Aldo Leopold, *A Sand County Almanac and Sketches Here and There* (New York: Oxford University Press, 1949), and Willard Savoy, *Alien Land* (New York: E. P. Dutton, 1949).

The examples cited on the Truman administration are described in Howard Zinn, "A People's War?" (chapter 16) and "Or Does It Explode?" (chapter 17) in *A People's History of the United States* (New York: Harper-Collins Perennial Classics, rev. 2001), 414, 425, 437. Lynching data come from the Tuskegee Institute.

On "moral consciousness is expanding more rapidly now than ever before . . .": J. Baird Callicott, "The Conceptual Foundations of the Land Ethic," in Callicott, ed., *Companion to* A Sand County Almanac: *Interpretive & Critical Essays* (Madison: University of Wisconsin Press, 1987), 188, 193.

In forty out of forty-four states with hazardous waste facilities, high percentages of people of color and the economically poor live, and die, next to those sites. See Robert Bullard and others, *Toxic Waste and Race at Twenty, 1987–2007: Grassroots Struggles to Dismantle Environmental Racism in the United States* (Cleveland, OH: United Church of Christ, 2007). http://www.ucc.org/justice/pdfs/toxic20.pdf.

On the goals and definitions of science: Aldo Leopold, "The State of the Profession," *Journal of Wildlife Management*, v. 4, 1940 (Also in Curt Meine, *Correction Lines: Essays on Land, Leopold, and Conservation* [Washington DC: Island Press, 2004], 149, 269.) Leopold quote from "Conservation" appears in *Round River: From the Journals of Aldo Leopold* (New York: Oxford University Press, 1993), 155.

E. O. Wilson, *The Diversity of Life* (New York: W. W. Norton & Company, 1999 [2nd edition]), 348.

J. Saunders Redding, *On Being Negro in America.* Frantz Fanon, *Black Skin, White Masks.* James Baldwin, *The Fire Next Time.* Herbert Hill, ed., *Anger, and Beyond: The Negro Writer in America.*

Viktor Frankl, *Man's Search for Meaning: An Introduction to Logotherapy* (Boston: Beacon Press, 1959; reprinted by Pocket Books, 1997), 213–14, 172, 104, 166.

MADELINE TRACES

The naming of Great Lakes in George Stewart, *Names on the Land: A Historical Account of Place-Naming in the United States*, 3rd ed. (Boston: Houghton Mifflin Company, 1967), 82–83.

Gerald Vizenor remembers Madeline Island as tribal home: Gerald Vizenor, "Shadows at La Pointe" in *Touchwood* (St. Paul: New Rivers Press, 1987), 130; and Gerald Vizenor, *People Named Chippewa: Narrative Histories* (Minneapolis: University of Minnesota Press, 1984), 47.

Vizenor describes how "people measured life in the circles of the sun and moon and human heart": Gerald Vizenor, *Everlasting Sky* (St. Paul, MN: Minnesota Historical Society Press, 1972), 6.

The Anishinaabe did not name themselves Ojibwa or Chippewa: Vizenor, *Everlasting Sky*, 8; the "*anishinabe* must still wear the invented names," *Everlasting Sky*, 10.

On Schoolcraft as "a highly versatile man": Charles R. McCullough, "Jane Schoolcraft Monument," reprinted from *Hamilton Spectator* [Ontario] in *Michigan History Magazine*, v. 30, n. 2 (1946), 386–92.

Mary Howard, the second Mrs. Henry R. Schoolcraft, wrote these words in her book, *The Black Gauntlet: A Tale of Plantation Life in South Carolina* (Philadelphia: J. B. Lippincott & Co., 1860).

"This Indian Edda—if I may so call it": Henry Wadsworth Longfellow, *The Works of Henry Wadsworth Longfellow, Volume 2* (Boston: Houghton, Mifflin, 1910), 851–52.

Longfellow preferred Hiawatha: "I chose it instead of Manabozho (Ojibway) for the sake of euphony": Alan Trachtenberg, *Shades of Hiawatha: Staging Indians, Making Americans, 1880–1930* (New York: Hill and Wang, 2005), 81.

Translations and the "internationalization" of *The Song of Hiawatha*: Joe Lockard, "The Universal Hiawatha," *American Indian Quarterly*, v. 24 (Winter 2000), 110–25. Bunin and Tschernichowsky quotes, p. 116. Canadian Pacific Railroad play, p. 120.

Daniel Aaron introduction to Everyman Library edition of *The Song of Hiawatha*: Henry Wadsworth Longfellow, 1855, *The Song of Hiawatha*, ed. by Daniel Aaron (London: Everyman Library, J. M. Dent, 1992), xii, xvi, xviii.

Gerald Vizenor has described the "shadow name" of the woodland trickster of the Anishinaabe: Gerald Vizenor, *Manifest Manners: Narratives on Postindian Survivance* (Lincoln: University of Nebraska Press, 1994), 170.

James Madison letter to Thomas McKenney: Richard Drinnon, *Facing West: The Metaphysics of Indian-Hating and Empire-Building* (Norman: University of Oklahoma Press, 1997), 182.

Thomas McKenney on Fond du Lac treaty and Lewis Cass: Drinnon, *Facing West*, 169–70. For more on Cass see also Zinn, *A People's History*, 132.

The texts of treaties are available online. The 1826 Fond du Lac treaty, for example, can be found at http://digital.library.okstate.edu/kappler/vol2/treaties/chi0268.htm. For information on the sequence of treaties, see Ronald Satz, *Chippewa Treaty Rights: The Reserved Rights of Wisconsin's Chippewa Indians in Historical Perspective* (Madison: Wisconsin Academy of Sciences, Arts and Letters, 1991).

"I have nothing to say about the Treaty . . .": Words spoken by Chief Buffalo to Subagent Daniel Bushnell, December 10, enclosed in Superintendent of Indian Affairs Henry Dodge to Commissioner of Indian Affairs C. A. Harris, February 19, 1838. Office of Indian Affairs, *Letters Sent, La Pointe Agency*, Microcopy 234, Roll 387, Record Group 75. Washington, DC: National Archives and Records Administration. Text in Satz, *Chippewa Treaty Rights*, 31.

The 1842 La Pointe treaty text: http://digital.library.okstate.edu/kappler/vol2/treaties/chi0542.htm.

"Great Father" in Washington "knows that you are poor . . .": Words spoken by treaty commissioner Robert Stuart in Satz, *Chippewa Treaty Rights*, 37.

The 1854 treaty text: http://digital.library.okstate.edu/kappler/vol2/treaties/chi0648.htm.

Families of the crane: Gerald Vizenor, *Interior Landscapes: Autobiographical Myths and Metaphors* (Minneapolis: University of Minnesota Press, 1990), 3–20.

One source on the history of dynamics between the Anishinaabe of the Red Cliff and Bad River reservations and the National Park Service is

Robert H. Keller and Michael Turek, *American Indians and National Parks* (Tucson: University of Arizona Press, 1998), 3–16.

For author Louise Erdrich the painted islands: Louise Erdrich, *Books and Islands in Ojibwe Country: Traveling Through the Land of My Ancestors* (Washington, DC: National Geographic Society, 2003), 86.

For some like Lt. Henry Wolsey Bayfield: Commander Henry W. Bayfield, "Outlines of the Geology of Lake Superior," *Transactions of the Literary and Historical Society of Quebec*, v. I., (1829), 4.

Charles R. Van Hise and Charles K. Leith, *The Geology of the Lake Superior Region* (Washington, DC: Government Printing Office, U.S. Geological Survey, 1911).

On the ceded lands leading the world in copper mined: Robert Keller, "An economic history of Indian treaties in the Great Lakes Region," *American Indian Journal*, v. 4 (February 1978), 2–20.

Gerald Vizenor has called their discoveries "the very cause of absence not the presence of natives": Gerald Vizenor, *Fugitive Poses: Native American Indian Scenes of Absence and Presence* (Lincoln: University of Nebraska Press, 1998), 84.

"The shadows of tribal names and stories are the ventures of landscapes": Vizenor, *Manifest Manners: Narratives on Postindian Survivance*, 10.

Constance Fenimore Woolson, *Anne* (New York: Harper & Brothers, 1882), 7–8.

WHAT'S IN A NAME

"Names are magic. One word can pour such a flood through the soul": Walt Whitman, "An American Primer," *The Atlantic Monthly*, v. 93, No. 558 (April, 1904), 460–70. http://www.theatlantic.com/past/docs/issues/04apr/primer.htm.

Erwin Raisz, *Landforms Map of the United States*, 6th ed., 1957, hand-drawn map to accompany Wallace Atwood, *The Physiographic Provinces of North America* (Boston: Ginn and Company, 1940). (Raisz's maps can be found at www.raiszmaps.com). Barry Lopez also notes, in his introduction to *Home Ground: Language for an American Landscape*, that he was drawn to the map through a youthful encounter. To him the language of place-names "radiates a sense of belonging."

Stewart's book *Storm* (1941) inspired the naming practices of military meteorologists during the Second World War. It later prompted the U.S. Weather Bureau (now the National Weather Service) to designate tropical storms with easily remembered first names of women. The story goes that Lerner and Loewe were inspired to pen "They Call the Wind Maria" for their musical *Paint Your Wagon*. That song, too, was another favorite from my childhood.

"Thus the names lay thickly over the land": Stewart, *Names on the Land*, 3–4.

Wallace Stegner, "George R. Stewart and the American Land" in *Where the Bluebird Sings to the Lemonade Springs: Living and Writing in the West* (New York: Penguin Books, 1992), 170, 171.

The introduction to the *New York Review of Books* edition: Matt Weiland, "Introduction" to Stewart, *Names on the Land*, ix–x, xii.

On "the names became more European than Indian": Stewart, *Names on the Land*, 10.

On "when tribes and languages had vanished": Stewart, *Names on the Land*, 3.

On the naming of San Francisco and Los Angeles: Stewart, *Names on the Land*, 156–57, 159–61.

"They left the land, as H. L. Mencken put it, 'bespattered with *Washingtons, Lafayettes, Jeffersons* and *Jacksons*'": H. L. Mencken, *The American Language: An Inquiry into the Development of English in the United States* (New York: A. A. Knopf, 1921).

On ideas of mapping: Karen Piper, *Cartographic Fictions: Maps, Race, and Identity* (New Brunswick: Rutgers University Press, 2002).

Massachusett, to the Wampanoag, means "place of the foothill": Wôpanâak Language Reclamation Project, personal communication.

Dakota, Illini, Kansa, Ute: Jack Weatherford, "The Naming of North America" (chapter 15) in *Native Roots: How the Indians Enriched America* (New York: Ballantine Books, 1992), 218.

On the origin of the name Wisconsin: Stewart, *Names on the Land*, 88.

On the naming of the Platte River: Stewart, *Names on the Land*, 136.

On the naming of the Appalachians: David Walls, "On the Naming of Appalachia," from *An Appalachian Symposium: Essays Written in Honor of Cratis D. Williams*, edited by J. W. Williamson (Boone, NC: Appalachian State University Press, 1977), 56–76; Stewart, *Names on the Land*, 17–18, 334; Davis, Donald E., *Where There Are Mountains: An Environmental History of the Southern Appalachians* (Athens, GA: University of Georgia Press, 2000), 3–5, 215–216; Jack Weatherford, *Native Roots*, 224. Note that the above authors, including Stewart, mistakenly state that Guyot's map used "Allegheny." The map used

"Alleghany" and can be seen in Arnold Guyot, "On the Appalachian Mountain System," *American Journal of Science*, Second Series, v. XXXI, n. 92 (1861), 157–187.

Arnold Guyot was a Swiss-born professor of geology and geography at Princeton University: William Libbey Jr., "The Life and Scientific Work of Arnold Guyot," *Journal of the American Geographical Society of New York*, v. 16 (1884) 194–221; Dana, James D., "Memoir of Arnold Guyot, 1807–1884" in *Biographical Memoirs*, v. ii (Washington, DC: National Academy of Sciences, 1886), 309–47; Walls, "On the Naming of Appalachia," 66; Stewart, *Names on the Land*, 334.

On the naming of Oregon: Stewart, *Names on the Land*, 153–155.

The 1809 poem "Gertrude of Wyoming" was written by Scottish poet Thomas Campbell. On the naming of Wyoming: Stewart, *Names on the Land*, 310–14.

See chapter 3, "Geographical Names," in Mencken, *The American Language*.

The U.S. Board on Geographic Names was established by executive order in 1890. See http://geonames.usgs.gov/.

The Wampanoag Nation's Wôpanâak Language Reclamation Project: The language of Wampanoag in Massachusetts had not been spoken in more than 150 years, six generations, yet the Wampanoag Nation is reclaiming it because theirs was also among the first Native languages to develop and use an alphabetic writing system, through the efforts of English missionaries trying to convert the Wampanoag to Christianity in the 1600s. The first complete bible printed in New England, and possibly the "new world," was published in the Wampanoag language in 1663. The Wampanoag came to use writing as the means of communicating with the European colonists. See http://wlrp.org/.

Many authors, including David Abram and Leslie Marmon Silko, have written of the land as the "matrix of linguistic meaning."

On "the continuity and accuracy of oral narratives": Leslie Marmon Silko, "Interior and Exterior Landscapes: The Pueblo Migration Stories," in *Yellow Woman and the Beauty of Spirit: Essays on Native American Life Today* (New York: Simon & Schuster, 1996), 35.

On Western Apache place-names and place-making: Keith Basso, *Wisdom Sits in Places* (Albuquerque: University of New Mexico Press, 1996), 76, 89, 45–46, 7.

The Apache word *ni'* means both land and mind: John Welch and Ramon Riley, "Reclaiming Land and Spirit in the Western Apache Homeland," *The American Indian Quarterly*, v. 25, n. 1 (Winter 2001), 5.

N. Scott Momaday, "Native American Attitudes to the Environment," in *Seeing with a Native Eye: Essays on Native American Religion*, ed. Walter Holden Capps (New York: Harper & Row, 1976), 80.

George Stewart concluded "the oppressed African left little mark upon the map": Stewart, *Names on the Land*, 329.

On African origins of place-names: Annette Kashif, "Africanisms upon the Land: A Study of African Influenced Place Names of the USA," in *Places of Cultural Memory: African Reflections on the American Landscape*. Conference Proceedings, May 9–12, 2001, Atlanta, GA. (Washington, DC: Department of the Interior, National Park Service, 15–34, http://www.cr.nps.gov/crdi/conferences/afr_15-34_kashif.pdf); Winifred Vass, *The Bantu Speaking Heritage of the United States* (Los Angeles: Center for Afro-American Studies, University of California, 1979); W. Vass, "Bantu Place Names in Nine Southern States" in Joseph Holloway and Winifred Vass, *African Heritage of American English* (Bloomington: University of Indiana Press, 1993).

On the origins of *Suwannee*: William Read, *Florida Place Names of Indian Origin and Seminole Personal Names* (Louisiana State University Press, 1934); Kashif, "Africanisms upon the Land," 19, 26; Vass, *African Heritage of American English*, 116, 134.

At least one maroon refuge lay in the Great Dismal Swamp straddling Virginia and North Carolina's low-country border. Note that the name is redundant, for *dismal* refers to dreary tracts of swamp.

Examples of hybrids or "creolizations" of African, Indigenous, and/or European languages may include Black Mingo Pocosin, a swamp along the Virginia–North Carolina border, according to Kashif, 27.

Several place-names once thought to be solely of Indigenous origin, or of dubious or unknown origins, may at least in part be rooted in Africa. Wando River in the Gullah region of South Carolina, for example, resembles the Kongo word *Kwando*, a large river (and a city on its banks) in Angola.

On Black towns in the West: Quintard Taylor, *In Search of the Racial Frontier: African Americans in the American West, 1528–1990* (New York: W. W. Norton, 1998), 69.

See U.S. Board of Geographic Names at http://geonames.usgs.gov/ to find the use of racial slurs in place-names.

PROPERTIES OF DESIRE

I learned later that the poet Lucille Clifton had a similar experience at Walnut Grove as the only person of color on a tour in 1989. The silence she experienced about slavery prompted her to write the poem "at the cemetery, walnut grove plantation, South Carolina, 1989."

Project Discovery Lesson 22 "Upstate Visit to Walnut Grove Plantation": http://www.knowitall.org/InstantReplay/files/pdr_walnut/Walnut%20Grove.pdf.

On colonial South Carolina and slavery: Winthrop Jordan, *White Over Black: American Attitudes toward the Negro 1550–1812* (Chapel Hill: University of North Carolina Press, 1968); Peter Wood, *Strange New Land: Africans in Colonial America* (Oxford: Oxford University Press, 2003); Ira Berlin, *Many Thousands Gone: The First Two Centuries of Slavery in America* (Cambridge, MA: Belknap Press of Harvard University Press, 1998); Peter Wood, *Black Majority: Negroes in Colonial South Carolina from 1670 through the Stono Rebellion* (New York: W. W. Norton & Company, 1996).

Some colonists also encouraged Native trading partners to raid neighboring villages for captives to be shipped to the Indies for profit: Daniel Richter, *Facing East from Indian Country: A Native History of Early America* (Cambridge, MA: Harvard University Press, 2001).

Remark by Samuel Dyssli in 1737 that "Carolina looks more like a negro country than like a country settled by white people": Wood, *Strange New Land*, 39.

George Washington worried if "that man is not crushed by spring, he will become the most formidable enemy America has": Wood, *Strange New Land*, 93.

Ira Berlin discusses fugitive slaves in the Lower South during Revolution, their fleeing on British vessels, the growth of cotton, and South Carolina's importing nearly ninety thousand Africans in *Generations of Captivity* (Cambridge, MA: Belknap Press of Harvard University Press, 2003), 124–26, 130–31; and *Many Thousands Gone*, 290–316.

Governor Montagu observation in 1772 about "producing luxuriantly Indigo, Hemp, Tobacco, and all English Grains": A. S. Salley, "The

Boundary Line between North and South Carolina," *Bulletins of the Historical Commission of South Carolina*, No. 10 (1929), 30. Also in Spartanburg Unit of the Writers' Program of the Work Projects Administration in the State of South Carolina, *A History of Spartanburg County* (Spartanburg, SC: Band & White, 1940; The Reprint Company, Publishers, American Guide Series, 1976), 18.

Thomas Moore's hospitality: *A History of Spartanburg County*, 45–46.

On the growth of cotton after the Revolution: Berlin, *Many Thousands Gone*, 307, 310; *Generations of Captivity*, 127, 130.

On the number of enslaved persons in the upcountry tripling between 1790 and 1810: Rachel Klein, *Unification of a Slave State: The Rise of the Planter Class in the South Carolina Backcountry, 1760–1808* (Chapel Hill: University of North Carolina Press), 253.

On New Englanders setting up first cotton mills on the Tyger River between 1816 and 1818: *A History of Spartanburg County*, 73.

On Philip Weaver, Rhode Island native and cotton factory owner, choosing to depart: "I wish to leave this part of the country and wish to settle myself and family in a free state": *A History of Spartanburg County*, 75.

On cotton cultivation and the demographics of Spartanburg "slave holdings" in 1860: Thomas Moore Craig, ed., *Upcountry South Carolina Goes to War: Letters of the Anderson, Brockman, and Moore Families, 1853–1865* (Columbia, SC: University of South Carolina Press, 2009), xiii, xv; W. J. Megginson, *African American Life in South Carolina's Upper Piedmont, 1780–1900* (Columbia, SC: University of South Carolina Press, 2006), 7.

February 1860 letter from Andrew C. Moore to his mother: Thomas Moore Craig, ed., *Upcountry South Carolina Goes to War*, 26. For Thomas Moore's 1866 "labor and commodity inventory" and labor contract, see 173–79.

South Carolina's Black Code of 1865: Lou Falkner Williams, *The Great South Carolina Ku Klux Klan Trials, 1871–1872* (Athens: University of Georgia Press, 1996), 3.

Spartanburg reaction to suspension of Black Code: *A History of Spartanburg County*, 141.

Ku Klux Klan in the Piedmont: Williams, *The Great South Carolina Ku Klux Klan Trials*, 15–49, 113, 126. For quote: "a heap goes to the penotensuary & all that is convicted for stealing is done voting" see 38.

See also *A History of Spartanburg County*, 141, 151; also Eric Foner, *Reconstruction: America's Unfinished Revolution* (New York: Harper & Row, 1988), 431.

On the Black Southside community in Spartanburg: Beatrice Lee and Brenda Hill, eds., *South of Main* (Spartanburg, SC: Hub City Press, 2005).

Historic Deerfield "is an outdoor history museum": http://www.historic-deerfield.org/discover-deerfield/village-overview/.

On slavery in Deerfield, Massachusetts: Robert Romer, *Slavery in the Connecticut Valley of Massachusetts* (Amherst, MA: Levellers Press, 2009). George Sheldon wrote the 1895 *History of Deerfield*.

"There shall never be any bond-slavery, villenage or captivitie amongst us": Jordan, *White Over Black*, 67.

See http://brown.edu/Facilities/John_Carter_Brown_Library/jcbexhibit/Pages/exhibAfricans.html for text of John Carter Brown Library exhibition "Africans in Colonial New England," which includes notes on the Pequot War and Winthrop's words on imported Africans. See also C. S. Manegold, *Ten Hills Farm: The Forgotten History of Slavery in the North* (Princeton: Princeton University Press, 2010).

"If upon a Just warre the Lord should deliver them into our hands" (Emanuel Downing's 1645 letter arguing for slave trade): Jordan, *White Over Black*, 69.

"To a large degree it may be said that Americans bought their independence with slave labor": Edmund S. Morgan, *American Slavery, American Freedom: The Ordeal of Virginia* (New York: W. W. Norton, 1975), 5.

"Cotton thread holds the union together": Ralph Waldo Emerson, *The Heart of Emerson's Journals* (Mineola, NY: Dover Publications, 2012, edited by Bliss Perry), 219–20.

Fernando Wood on the NYC secession: *New York Times* (January 8, 1861), 4. Discussion in Tyler G. Anbinder, "Fernando Wood and New York City's Secession from the Union: A Political Appraisal," *New York History*, v. 68 (January 1987). Also in Anne Farrow, Joel Lang, and Jenifer Frank, *Complicity: How the North Promoted, Prolonged, and Profited from Slavery* (New York: Ballantine Books, 2005), 3–4.

The privilege and profits slavery afforded reside not only in the past: Farrow, Lang, and Frank, *Complicity*; Alan J. Singer, *New York and Slavery: Time to Teach the Truth* (Albany: State University of New

York Press, 2008); Craig S. Wilder, *Ebony and Ivy: Race, Slavery, and the Troubled History of America's Universities* (New York: Blooms-bury Press, 2013); *Slavery and Justice: Report of the Brown University Steering Committee on Slavery and Justice* (Providence: Brown University, 2006, updated 2011).

Bernard Bailyn, "Considering the slave trade: History and memory," *William and Mary Quarterly*, v. 58, no. 1 (2001), 245–52.

On public representations of slavery in the South: Jennifer Eichstedt and Stephen Small, *Representations of Slavery: Race and Ideology in Southern Plantation Museums* (Washington, DC: Smithsonian Books, 2002); W. Fitzhugh Brundage, *The Southern Past: A Clash of Race and Memory* (Cambridge, MA: Belknap Press of Harvard University Press, 2008); Paul Shackel, *Memory in Black and White: Race, Commemoration, and the Post-Bellum Landscape* (Walnut Creek, CA: AltaMira Press, 2003); David Blight, *Race and Reunion: The Civil War in American Memory* (Cambridge, MA: Belknap Press of Harvard University Press, 2002). Cane River Creole National Historical Park in Louisiana attempts to present facts and contexts at its Magnolia and Oakland plantations. North Carolina's Somerset Plantation has tried to help descendants of the enslaved and enslavers face their shared and divergent histories with annual reunions. These are exceptions.

Lesson 22's virtual field trip to Walnut Grove: https://www.yumpu.com/en/document/view/23593013/upstate-visit-to-walnut-grove-plantation.

On Disney's America: Mike Wallace, *Mickey Mouse History and Other Essays on American Memory* (Temple University Press, 1996), 163–64.

On Black landscapes on plantations: Rebecca Ginsberg, "Escaping through a Black Landscape," in Clifton Ellis and Rebecca Ginsberg, eds., *Cabin, Quarter, Plantation: Architecture and Landscapes of North American Slavery* (New Haven: Yale University Press, 2010), 51–66.

I'd withered far too much: Audre Lorde, "Eye to Eye: Black Women, Hatred, and Anger" in *Sister Outsider: Essays and Speeches* (Freedom, CA: The Crossing Press, 1984), 164.

MIGRATING IN A BORDERED LAND

In July 2013 a federal court ordered the Tucson Unified School District to reinstate "culturally relevant" courses, including Mexican American and

African American studies. The courses are offered through the school system's "Culturally Relevant Pedagogy and Instruction" program.

Origins of the San Pedro Ethnohistory Project (SPEP): Narratives of archaeologists, anthropologists, and historians in the last century tended to neglect the voices and views of the ancient peoples' descendants. T. J. Ferguson, Chip Colwell-Chanthaphonh, and colleagues recognized that a fuller, more respectful understanding of the San Pedro Valley's human presence needed multivocality in partnership and established the SPEP. See Ferguson and Colwell-Chanthaphonh, *History Is in the Land: Multivocal Tribal Traditions in Arizona's San Pedro Valley* (Tucson: University of Arizona Press, 2006).

The account describes my April 2012 visit to Montezuma Pass and the U.S.–Mexico Border at Naco.

Mexican War "unnecessary, impolitic, illegal, and immoral": John Schroeder, *Mr. Polk's War: American Opposition and Dissent, 1846–1848* (Madison: University of Wisconsin Press, 1973), xiv.

Colonel Ethan Allen Hitchcock: Zinn, chapter 8, "We Take Nothing by Conquest, Thank God," in *A People's History of the United States*; "Ethan Allen Hitchcock and the Mexican War Spy Company," Fort Huachuca History Program under "Masters of the Intelligence Art": http://www.huachuca.army.mil/files/History_MHITCH.PDF.

Mr. Polk argued that war existed "'notwithstanding all our efforts to avoid it" and that "Mexico has passed the boundary of the United States, has invaded our territory and shed American blood upon the American soil": Christopher Conway, ed., *The U.S.–Mexican War: A Binational Reader* (Indianapolis: Hackett Publishing Company, 2010), 60.

Frederick Douglass referred to the "disgraceful, cruel, and iniquitous" conflict as a "murderous war": Conway, *The U.S.–Mexican War*, 124–25.

John L. O'Sullivan called for "the fulfillment of our manifest destiny to overspread the continent allotted by Providence for the free development of our yearly multiplying millions": Conway, *The U.S.–Mexican War*, 53.

Henry David Thoreau later wrote in "Civil Disobedience": Henry David Thoreau, *The Portable Thoreau* (New York: Penguin Press, 2012).

Text of the Treaty of Guadalupe Hidalgo: http://avalon.law.yale.edu/19th_century/guadhida.asp#art11.

"Ours is the government of the white man," John C. Calhoun argued: Conway, *The U.S.–Mexican War*, 120–21.

To the *National Intelligencer,* Washington's Whig newspaper: February 29, 1848, in Schroeder, *Mr. Polk's War,* 157.

Even the U.S. treaty commissioner thought the map "suddenly got up. . .": Paula Rebert, *La Gran Línea: Mapping the United States–Mexico Boundary, 1849–1857* (Austin: University of Texas Press, 2001), 6.

The New York Herald called it "God-forsaken country": Amy Greenberg, "Domesticating the Border," in Alexis McCrossen, *Land of Necessity: Consumer Culture in the United States–Mexico Borderlands* (Durham: Duke University Press, 2010), 88.

Land grab corrupting political process by "South Carolina diplomacy": Greenberg, "Domesticating the Border," 88.

As they made and marked the "true line . . .": Rebert, *La Gran Línea,*185.

And by following the plan to "note the general character of the country . . .": Rebert, *La Gran Línea,* 28.

For years a railroad spike driven into the ground marked the border here at Naco: Michael Dear, *Why Walls Won't Work: Repairing the US-Mexico Divide* (Oxford: Oxford University Press, 2013), 13.

Juan de Oñate 1599 note about the Apache: George P. Hammond and Agapito Rey, eds., *Don Juan de Oñate: Colonizer of New Mexico, 1595–1628* (Albuquerque: University of New Mexico, 1953), v. 1, 484.

On names Janos, Jocomes, Sumas disappearing from Spanish records as the use of *Apache* became prominent: Jack D. Forbes, "Unknown Athapaskans: The Identification of the Jano, Jocome, Jumano, Manso, Suma, and Other Indian Tribes of the Southwest," *Ethnohistory,* v. 6, n. 2 (Spring 1959), 124. See also Ferguson and Colwell-Chanthaphonh, *History Is in the Land,* for discussion of Spanish-tribal interactions in the San Pedro Valley and nearby areas.

In his *Memorias sobre las Provincias del Norte de Nueva España* (1799): José Cortés, Lieutenant in the Royal Corps of Engineers, 1799, *Views from the Apache Frontier: Report on the North Provinces of New Spain,* edited by Elizabeth A. H. John, translated by John Wheat (Norman: University of Oklahoma Press, 1989), 28.

The "greater expertise and tactics" emerged from reforms set in place by Bernardo de Gálvez, Virrey (or Viceroy) de Nueva España, to sabotage traditional subsistence bases and autonomy of "Apache" groups.

For example, *indios de paz* cultivated the San Pedro Valley at Tres Alamos to supplement the Tucson presidio's food supply. See Ferguson and Colwell-Chanthaphonh, *History Is in the Land,* 201.

Scalp hunters determined to make money killed easier targets with straight black hair: Richard Perry, *Apache Reservation: Indigenous Peoples and the American State* (Austin: University of Texas Press, 1993), 85–87.

The legislature then sought help from the federal government "in subduing our hostile foe": Perry, *Apache Reservation*, 108.

Vincent Colyer made this note in his 1871–72 report on *Peace with the Apaches of New Mexico and Arizona.*

"Savage, treacherous and cruel as these Indians are," one officer noted in 1871: Ferguson and Colwell-Chanthaphonh, *History Is in the Land*, 205.

U.S. Army records and territorial newspapers of the time show that the number of Apaches killed in southern Arizona was many times that of Anglo casualties: Chip Colwell-Chanthaphonh, *Massacre at Camp Grant: Forgetting and Remembering Apache History* (Tucson: University of Arizona Press, 2007), 53; Ferguson and Colwell-Chanthaphonh, *History Is in the Land*, 204.

Colyer writes of his visit to the massacre site in "Condition of the Apache Indians—Camp Apache, White Mountains, Arizona" in *Annual Report of the Commissioner of Indian Affairs to the Secretary of the Interior for the Year 1871* (Washington, DC: Government Printing Office), 55.

"A rascal who comes here to thwart the attempts of military and citizens to conquer a peace from our savage foe, deserves to be stoned to death": Perry, *Apache Reservation*, 114.

"Violence may begin as a contest over resources . . .": Karl Jacoby, *Shadows at Dawn: An Apache Massacre and the Violence of History* (New York: Penguin Books, 2008), 4.

"If any one post of the United States Army might lay claim to being the home station of the Buffalo Soldiers . . .": Cornelius Smith, Jr., *Fort Huachuca: The Story of a Frontier Post* (Fort Huachuca, Arizona, 1976), 197.

On the growth of Fort Huachuca before and during the Second World War: Steven D. Smith, *The African American Soldier At Fort Huachuca, Arizona, 1892–1946* (Columbia, SC: University of South Carolina—South Carolina Institute of Archaeology and Anthropology, 2001).

Major General Edward Almond believed Southern officers at Fort Huachuca "understood the characteristic of the Negro and his habits and inclinations" and his "capabilities": Robert F. Jefferson, *Fighting for Hope: African American Troops of the 93rd Infantry Division in World War II and Postwar America* (Baltimore: Johns Hopkins University Press, 2008), 83, 269–70.

Commanding officer's response of "I hate niggers": Jefferson, *Fighting for Hope*, 83–84, 270.

Declassified complaints about and protests against discriminatory practices (e.g., rank ceiling and "inefficient officer school"), treatment of soldiers, racist incidents, and general conditions at Fort Huachuca were found at the National Archives and Records Administration, College Park, MD (NARA II): Record Group 107.2.8, Records of the Office of the Civilian Aide to the Secretary of War, Reports and memorandums on racial conditions in the U.S. Army; and Record 338, Records of Headquarters, Third U.S. Army/Adjutant General, 338.3 Entry 50473 General correspondence.

African American leaders in health fields had tried to persuade Surgeon General James C. Magee: Declassified "Minutes of meeting, 10 a.m., March 7, 1941 re: use of Negro doctors, nurses and dentists by Med. Dept." at NARA II, Record Group 112, Records of Office of Surgeon General, Entry 31ah WWII Admin Records 2I [Geographic File, 1917–49], Decimal file 291.2 390 16/08/04, Box 199.

"For the first time in the history of the army opportunity has been furnished the Negro medical profession": Undersecretary of War Robert Patterson cited in Darlene Clark Hine, *Black Women in White: Racial Conflict and Cooperation in the Nursing Profession 1890–1950* (Bloomington: Indiana University Press, 1989), 166.

"We fail to understand how America can say to the World that in this country we are ready to defend democracy": Mabel Staupers cited in Darlene Clark Hine, "Mabel Staupers and the Integration of Black Nurses into the Armed Forces," in John Hope Franklin and August Meier, eds., *Black Leaders of the Twentieth Century* (Urbana: University of Illinois, 1982) 247.

"When our women hear of the great need for nurses in the Army": Mabel Staupers cited in Hine, *Black Women in White*, 178.

Lieutenant Colonel Roscoe C. Giles was the first African American to graduate from Cornell University's medical school and the first certified by the American Board of Surgery. Major William E. Allen was the first African American to be certified in radiology by the American Board of

Radiology and the first elected by the American College of Radiology as a Fellow.

An inspector from the army's Medical Corps reported late in the war: Declassified "Report of Visit to Fort Huachuca" by Durward G. Hall, Colonel, Medical Corps at NARA II, Record Group 112, Records of Office of Surgeon General, Entry 29f , General Subject File (1943–44), Decimal file 291.2 390 14/26/04, Box 307.

African American nurses and German-born Jewish doctors cared for Nazi prisoners: Ralph A. Storm, *Camp Florence Days: A World War II Prisoner of War Camp* (self-published account by veteran stationed there during the war, 2006), 33–34.

Whether in Florence or Phoenix it was often the same greeting: Letter to Mrs. Mabel Staupers from nurse (1944 or 1945), NARA II Record Group 107, Records of the Office of the Civilian Aide to the Secretary of War, Box 225, "Nurses" file.

Staupers gathered that a problem larger than civilian prejudice "was the prejudice exhibited in camps": Mabel Keaton Staupers, *No Time for Prejudice: A Story of the Integration of Negroes in Nursing in the United States* (New York: The Macmillan Company, 1961), 116.

Nothing of the case of a young medical officer at Fort Huachuca who was court-martialed: Jefferson, *Fighting for Hope*, 84, 270.

On segregated service clubs at Fort Huachuca: Smith, *The African American Soldier At Fort Huachuca,* 133–35.

On eligibility of Building 66050 for the National Register of Historic Places: Matt C. Bischoff, *Determination of Eligibility and Historical Documentation for Building 66050, Performing Arts Theater, Fort Huachuca, Arizona* (Tucson: Statistical Research, Inc. Technical Report 98–26).

Self-titled and self-invented "Colonel" William Greene made his mark on both sides as a promoter and venturer in cattle ranching and mining. His copper mines by the San Pedro's headwaters in Sonora—the Cananea Consolidated Copper Company—had become a fifty-million-dollar business by the first decade of the twentieth century. Discontented Mexican workers went on strike there in 1906 for wages and treatment closer to what Americans there received. Their walkout and the subsequent riot would supply one of the early sparks to the Mexican Revolution.

PLACING WASHINGTON, D.C., AFTER THE INAUGURATION

On the siting of Washington, DC: Garry Wills, "Seat of Bondage," *American Heritage*, v. 54, n. 6 (2003), 57–62; Garry Wills, *The Negro President: Jefferson and the Slave Power* (New York: Houghton Mifflin Company, 2003), 204–13; Don E. Fehrenbacher, *The Slaveholding Republic: An Account of the United States Government's Relations to Slavery* (New York: Oxford University Press, 2001); Herbert Sloan, *Principle and Interest: Thomas Jefferson and the Debt* (Charlottesville: University Press of Virginia, 1995), 125–26, 225–32; Keith Melder, "Slaves and Freedmen," *The Wilson Quarterly*, v. 13, n. 1, (1989), 76–83.

Chesapeake tobacco exports exploded: For example, Alvin Rabushka, *Taxation in Colonial America* (Princeton, NJ: Princeton University Press, 2010), 229–30; *Historical Statistics of the United States, Colonial Times to 1970, Parts 1–2* (Washington, DC: U.S. Department of Commerce, Bureau of the Census, 1975), 1162–63.

On owners of capital land: John Michael Vlach, "The Quest for a Capital," The Ruth Ann Overbeck Capitol Hill History Project Lecture Series, 2003, http://capitolhillhistory.org/lectures/vlach/; John Michael Vlach, "The Mysterious Mr. Jenkins of Jenkins Hill: The Early History of the Capitol Site," Washington, DC: U.S. Capitol Historical Society, 2004, http://capitolhillhistory.org/library/04/Jenkins%20Hill.html.

On foreign visitors to Washington: The quotes from Charles Dickens and Harriet Martineau appear in John W. Reps, *Washington on View: The Nation's Capital since 1790* (Chapel Hill, NC: University of North Carolina Press, 1991); also Harriet Martineau, *Retrospect of Western Travel* (London: Saunders and Otley, 1838). http://www.archive.org/details/retrospectofwest02martrich.

Frederick Douglass words on the siting of the District of Columbia as mistake: http://www.loc.gov/teachers/classroommaterials/connections/capital-bay/history4.html.

Records of the Commissioners for the District of Columbia directed compensation: William C. Allen, History of Slave Laborers in the Construction of the United States Capitol (Washington, DC: Office of the Architect of the Capitol, 2005). http://artandhistory.house.gov/art_artifacts/slave_labor_reportl.pdf.

Many references exist on "slave" pens, slavery, and the District of Columbia trade: For example, Federal Writers' Project, *Washington, City and Capitol* (Washington, DC: U.S. Government Printing Office, Works

Progress Administration American Guide Series, 1937), 69; Steven Deyle, *Carry Me Back: The Domestic Slave Trade in American Life* (New York: Oxford University Press, 2005); Constance Green, *The Secret City: A History of Race Relations in the Nation's Capital* (Princeton, NJ: Princeton University Press, 1967); Mary Beth Corrigan, "Imaginary Cruelties?: A History of the Slave Trade in Washington, D.C.," *Washington History: Magazine of the Historical Society of Washington, D.C.*, v. 13 (Fall/Winter 2001–2002), 4–27.

President Madison's private secretary, Edward Coles, reproached his employer: Ralph Ketcham, "The Dictates of Conscience: Edward Coles and Slavery," *Virginia Quarterly Review*, v. 36, 52.

On the "secret city" of free and enslaved African Americans in the capital and Black codes: Green, *The Secret City*; Letitia Woods Brown, *Free Negroes in the District of Columbia* (New York: Oxford University Press, 1972); Hilary Russell, "The Operation of the Underground Railroad in Washington, D.C., c. 1800–1860" (Final Research Report of the Historical Society of Washington D.C. and the National Park Service, 2001); Kate Masur, *An Example for All the Land: Emancipation and the Struggle over Equality in Washington, D.C.* (Chapel Hill: University of North Carolina Press, 2010).

In the spring of 1831 a large group gathered at the African Methodist Episcopal Church formally declared that "the soil that gave us birth is our only true and veritable home": Green, *The Secret City*, 34.

"We have already too many free negroes and mulattoes in this city": Green, *The Secret City*, 37.

Elizabeth Savoy and Underground Railroad in Henry S. Robinson, "Some Aspects of the Free Negro Population of Washington, D.C., 1800–1862," *Maryland Historical Magazine*, v. 64, n. 1 (1969), 61.

Woodlawn cemetery: Paul Sluby, *Woodlawn Cemetery, Washington, D.C.*, (Temple Hills, MD: Comprehensive Research, revised 2006); P. Sluby, *Bury Me Deep: Burial Places Past and Present in and nearby Washington, D.C.: A Historical Review and Reference Manual* (Temple Hills, MD: Comprehensive Research, 2012).

On October 16, 2013, Congresswoman Eleanor Holmes Norton (D-DC) read a statement for the Congressional Record, announcing the "Clean up our History Day at Woodlawn Cemetery" on October 19. Norton said, "I ask the House to join me as we recognize the volunteers from the District of Columbia National Guard, Woodlawn Cemetery

Perpetual Care Association, and families of loved ones interred at Woodlawn for their participation in the kickoff of the cleanup of historic Woodlawn Cemetery as we begin an effort to restore the cemetery to its rightful place on the historical map for the benefit of families, historians, scholars and visitors, and cast light on one of the most important periods in African American history." I hope the efforts can continue.

EPILOGUE: AT CROWSNEST PASS

S. Conway Morris, L. E. Savoy, and A. G. Harris, "An Enigmatic Organism from the 'Exshaw' Formation (Devonian-Carboniferous), Alberta, Canada," *Lethaia*, v. 24, 139–152.

INDEX